Faces of Hiroshima

Faces of Hiroshima

A Report by
Anne Chisholm

JONATHAN CAPE
THIRTY-TWO BEDFORD SQUARE LONDON

To my god-daughters:
Sarah, Tamsin, Martha, Lucy,
Charlotte and Amy

23774
940.5'25
C 45

First published 1985
Copyright © by Anne Chisholm 1985
Jonathan Cape Ltd, 32 Bedford Square, London WC1B 3EL

British Library Cataloguing in Publication Data
Chisholm, Anne
Faces of Hiroshima: a report.
1. World War, 1939–1945 – Personal narratives, Japanese – Case studies
2. Hiroshima-shi (Japan) – Bombardment, 1945 – Case studies
I. Title
940.54'25   D767.25.H6
ISBN 0–224–02831–6
ISBN 0–224–02836–7 Pbk

Printed in Great Britain by Butler and Tanner Ltd
Frome and London

Contents

Preface   vii

Part 1: Japan, 1945–53   1

  1 'A Bomb Has Dropped'   3
  2 Hiroshima Consumed   12
  3 After the Bombing   23
  4 'A New Ugly Me'   31
  5 Seeking Help   41

Part 2: America, 1953–6   55

  6 The Hiroshima Maidens Project   57
  7 The Group Is Chosen   73
  8 From Hiroshima to New York   83
  9 Surgery   99
 10 'Just a Stupid Accident'   115

Part 3: Japan and America, 1956–85   125

 11 Aftermath in Hiroshima   127
 12 The Risk of Marriage   134
 13 Jobs and Jealousies   142
 14 Shigeko in Manhattan Beach   151
 15 Forty Years Later   160
 16 In Hiroshima Now   173

Postscript   180

Note on Sources   182

Preface

I first learned of the existence of the twenty-five women known as the Hiroshima Maidens from a short article I read last year in an English-language Tokyo newspaper. These women, most of them schoolgirls in 1945, had been among the many who were badly burned and disfigured in the atomic bombing of Hiroshima. Ten years later, they were selected by a group of Americans as suitable recipients of treatment and taken to the United States for plastic surgery. Thirty years later, some of them were said to be still scarred physically and mentally, and reluctant to talk about their experiences.

I had recently visited Hiroshima and been moved and appalled by the Peace Museum and its exhibits. It struck me how vague and inaccurate most people's knowledge still is of the precise effects of the world's first atomic bombing. We are even more ignorant about how those who survived the bombing have lived since, and about how they feel today. I found I wanted to learn more about this particular group of women, and about the genesis and outcome of the Hiroshima Maidens project. Although the women were said to avoid outsiders I hoped that some of them might agree to talk to a woman not far from them in age, and neither Japanese nor American. From England, I contacted the only journalist to have reached them, with difficulty, in recent years: Kazuo Chujo, himself a survivor of Hiroshima. I asked if he would help me; he agreed.

Some people, I have discovered, feel that to pursue the details of what happened at Hiroshima and afterwards is evidence of a prurient urge to dwell on past horrors. To retell the story at all is taken to mean that one must be a convinced unilateralist or CND activist. Others deny that the bombing of Hiroshima was very different from any act of war inflicted on civilians, and seek to remind one of other atrocities, some perpetrated by the Japanese. I am aware that all wars leave scars on people's minds and bodies: but the first scars of the nuclear age seem to me to be especially significant. My purposes in pursuing the Hiroshima Maidens' story and talking to the women themselves were simple. I believed that these women could help us to understand some important matters. They could say not only what it was like to be burned in an atomic explosion, but what it was like to live on as an involuntary symbol of the world's first experience of nuclear war. Through them, and their relations with those Americans who tried to help them, the uneasy conscience of the country that dropped the first bomb might be suggested. Above all, I wanted to let the women themselves, and some of those close to them, tell us about their lives over the last forty years.

Since 1945 a considerable body of writing and drama has grown up around events at Hiroshima and Nagasaki. Survivors have told their stories, and these have been re-created in novels and films, both documentary and imagined. However, it is still easy to avoid confronting the truth of what happened – either because it is too painful or because it does not quite fit the legends or theories. Fiction and drama are often distorting. The facts cannot be examined too often: I agree with Martha Gellhorn, the writer and war correspondent, that 'Memory and imagination, not nuclear weapons, are the great deterrents.'

This account concentrates on what happened to a small group of Hiroshima survivors. I have not attempted a general account of the bombing or its consequences but I have tried to put the story in context. I have interviewed as many as I could reach of those concerned with the Hiroshima Maidens project, starting in the United States and going on to Japan. I know no Japanese; most of the women I interviewed had very limited English. With them, I used an interpreter, but have quoted them in the text as if they spoke directly to me. With three, however, I talked in English, which they knew reasonably well. I have not corrected their small errors; their use of the language is graphic and moving, and our efforts at mutual comprehension often seemed to me to be part of the story.

Above all, I would like to thank the women from Hiroshima who overcame their reluctance to relive the past and agreed to talk to me. As some of them did not wish to be easily identifiable I have used only their first names in the text, adding an initial when two women share a name, and shall not list them here.

I am also extremely grateful to Kazuo Chujo, who with great generosity shared his experiences, his material and his insights with me. Mieko Yasuhara was an exemplary interpreter and colleague. Their help was invaluable. My thanks also go to the following:

In America: Jean Anderson, Carlyn and Colin Chisholm, Ellen and Norman Cousins, Ida and Richard Day, Robert Hughes, Robert Jay and Betty Jean Lifton, Ellen Mensch, Dr Bernard Simon, Deborah and Robert Teel.

In Japan: Dr Tomin Harada, Claire and George Hughes, Peter and Emiko McGill, Zen Matsutani, Seimei Murata, Hiroko Nakamoto, The Reverend and Mrs Tanimoto, Helen Yokoyama.

In England: Liz Calder, Michael Davie, Maggie Keswick, Susie and David Sainsbury, Jesse Stoecker, Donald Trelford.

London, March 1985   A.C.

Part 1

Japan, 1945–53

1

'A Bomb Has Dropped'

The women tell their stories quietly and simply, with a slight air of resignation. They smile politely as I apologise for re-opening a painful topic; they know that behind the concern lies a curiosity, even a need, to hear the horrifying details. These women know, too, that once their history is known, the scars on their faces and necks, visible despite the careful make-up, will be scrutinised with special interest. I am aware, too, of the more extensive scarring beneath the neat, conventional clothes. Some of the scars are unobtrusive, hardly noticeable in ordinary circumstances; others are prominent, ugly and distressing, embarrassing to look at and unimaginable to live with. I feel uneasy, torn between a wish to ignore the scars and the task of learning about their origin. The women's composure is remarkable, and unsettling. Crossing their ankles, folding their hands, leaning forward with an anxious, smiling politeness, eager to help, they reach back nearly forty years to tell how it happened.

Then, most of them were children. Now they are middle-aged women, very different from one another in temperament and circumstances, but still linked by their common experience of 6 August 1945 and what came after.

Shigeko is a small woman with quick movements, smiling and full of energy. The top half of her face is sunny and open, with unusually pretty dark eyes; she has long thick black hair, falling casually over her forehead and round her neck and shoulders. The lower half of her face, from a line running below her cheekbones across the middle of her upper lip, is different; the shape is lumpy and the texture looks hard and smooth. Her mouth, drawn in with dull pinkish-brown lipstick, is oddly shaped; the lips are not really lips. Her neck is badly scarred too, and her small hands are misshapen. They are clawlike, bent back at the wrists and base of the fingers. The skin on her hands is brownish, shiny in patches, and curiously plump. The nails are well kept, but some are deformed. Nevertheless her hands are extremely mobile and efficient and she uses them without awkwardness or self-consciousness. Her voice and expressions are full of spirit and gaiety. Sometimes her face, despite its scars, looks strikingly pretty; then suddenly it is as if something slips and she becomes ugly, but not for long.

We had been talking of other things; when I asked her to tell me what had happened to her on the morning of 6 August 1945 she readily agreed. But her voice became lower, more serious, and her expression anxious and intent.

I was thirteen years old; I was ordered into the centre of the city to clean up the streets. We were working about 1.6 kilometres from the hypocentre. I heard the aeroplane; I looked up at the sky – the plane had a pretty white tail, it was a sunny day, the sky was blue. This had happened many times before, so I didn't feel scared. Then I saw something drop – white I think – and pow! – a big explosion knocked me down.

Then I was unconscious – I don't know for how long. Then I was conscious but I couldn't see anything, it was all black and red. Then I called my friend, Toshiko; then the fog goes away but I can't find her. I never see her again. Then I see people moving away and I just follow them. It is not light like it was before, it is more like evening. I look around; houses are all flat! I could see straight, clear, all a long distance. I follow the people to the river. I couldn't hear anything, my ears are blocked up — or maybe my consciousness is blocked out. I am thinking — a bomb has dropped!

I heard a baby screaming — that woke me up and I could hear things, but nothing sounded loudly. Then I heard a man say, 'Let's go to the hills' — and I thought maybe I should go back to the school. People started to push; I was afraid I would fall into the water, and I wanted to leave with the others. There was an old woman on the ground and people were stepping on her. I couldn't help her up! [Shigeko held out her hands: tears came to her eyes.] I didn't know my hands were burned, nor my face. Very very difficult . . . all these years my regret . . . why couldn't I help her? It still hurts me.

Someone gave me oil for my hands and face. It hurt; my face had a swollen feeling, and I couldn't move my neck. My eyes were swollen and felt closed up. I got to my school yard and sat down, put my head back against a wall and — unconscious again. When I wake up — I don't know how long — it was so dark! I kept saying, 'Please give me some water; my name is Shigeko, I live at so and so, tell my parents I am here, my name is Shigeko, I live at so and so, tell my parents . . .' I thought if I say it once more someone will come and pick me up.

I don't know where I was; I was lying on the floor. I had been sitting outside but someone had carried me inside into the auditorium. All I remember is that I had walked into the school yard. Then four days later, my mother came. She had been in the house, which fell down and covered her with rubble, but she managed to get out. My father saw the plane too — he was working outside, and he said to a friend, 'Run!' He ran into a concrete ice box in the old fishmarket building, and so he was protected. When he came out all the others were burned. My father tried to organise help for people; my mother was looking for me every day. For four days, she searched for me, she even looked at dead bodies. My father told her on the fourth day, 'Don't go out again, you'll get sick.' But she sneaked out anyway.

That evening a man came and said he'd heard a voice at the school, a girl's voice so faint he could hardly hear, saying my name. My mother went out again with him, calling my name. I was unconscious; and I was dreaming of water. I saw a beautiful fountain, and the ocean all blue, blue, blue . . . I went into the beautiful blue . . . it was cool . . . I felt no suffering, no thirst, I felt light like a feather, not frightened any more. It was a joyful, happy feeling. No one was there, but a glow; just so happy . . . Then I heard my mother calling, 'Shigeko!' and I answered, 'I am here!' The next thing I knew, my mother was talking to a doctor, and I came back to myself. There was a sharp pain in my chest, and I had to have an injection for the heart. 'This girl has a strong heart,' someone said.

They put me on a wooden door with a blanket and took me home. I remember neighbours say, 'Oh! Shigeko came home! How nice!'

After that I was unconscious many many times and they thought I was dying. My mother had to listen to my heart. [Shigeko mimed an anxious listener, head cocked.] Still breathing! Still alive! This went on for perhaps two or three months. No, I don't remember pain very much. Physical pain you forget, like having a baby. Treatment? Just a little soy bean oil to clean up my face. My whole face was burned. I had no eyebrows. My mother had to pull my eyes open. When they tried to remove the burnt clothes, my skin came off as well. Four days later my father peeled the burned skin off my face. It was all black; underneath was like a cream puff, full of pus. He cut all my hair off because of the infection. But before, I had a little girl's haircut, with a fringe. [She held back her hair from her forehead, which is smooth and youthful still, and took my hand and placed it on the fine, soft skin.] You see?

Terue is a grandmother now and has a sensible, motherly look to her, with her round face, neatly curling short hair, gold teeth, and glasses. She appears hardly scarred at all. A flat patch of discoloured skin is faintly visible on her left cheek; there is a thin line below her mouth; and the area around her left eye is a little puckered. Like Shigeko, she was thirteen in August 1945.

> My mother had died of cancer two months earlier, and one member of the household had to go to work at an evacuation centre with the civilian volunteer groups; I was the only one free to go. We were all afraid of bombs because there had been continual air raid alerts; in fact there had been one just that morning, but then the all-clear sounded so we came out again from the shelters. I did not see the bomb falling but I saw a flash; then I felt my hair being singed by intense heat, and I lost consciousness. When I came to, everything was smouldering around me, dark and smoking, and I thought perhaps I was having a nightmare. Then I began to feel great pain; I was burned all over. I looked at my hands; they hurt, and the skin was hanging down. [She held out her hands and made a gesture like taking off a pair of gloves. Her hands look almost normal now, except for some scarring round the wrists.] I looked around: all the others looked the same.

Terue had been wearing a white cotton shirt with long sleeves that gave her arms some protection; but her trousers were of a synthetic material which melted, and her legs were badly burned. But she could walk, which surprises her now, and she began to move away blindly, not planning where she was going. Gradually she realised that it was once again a bright hot sunny day. The sunshine felt agonising on her raw flesh. A truck came past and someone pulled her up on to it; as it moved away she thought no, she must find her family, and slid off. Somehow, very slowly, she limped the four kilometres home. Her skin hung off in shreds and her hair was sticky with blood. She began to lose her sight; her left eyelid was burned away. She began to bump into things, which made her scream with pain. When she reached home, she could just see her father, himself covered with blood, in the ruins of their house. 'Father, it's me,' she said. She heard him say, hoarsely, 'What? You are Terue?' He told her afterwards that he could not recognise her; she was scorched black and her face was hugely swollen. Then she lost consciousness again.

Among the women I met, Terue was unusual in having vivid memories of feeling pain during the immediate aftermath of the explosion. For most of them, that came later; for all of them it was prolonged and intense, but what they recalled most clearly about the first hours was not pain so much as a stunned amazement, darkness and a muffled quiet.

Toyoko, at nineteen, was older than the others. Like them, she had started work early that morning with a demolition squad making fire-breaks for the bombings that Hiroshima was expecting. 'I don't remember very much,' she said, sitting in her tiny flat in the city centre, and serving me coffee and cookies. Classical music played on the radio in the background, and her miniature white poodle jumped around her feet.

The lower part of her face, including her nose, and her neck are still noticeably scarred, and her mouth is slightly distorted. 'I saw a wave of light, that was all. When I woke up I seemed to be alone. I felt no pain at all: I knew I could walk. But then you know, I touched my face and it was all swollen; and then I saw I had almost no clothes on. I started to walk away ... I followed sounds ... then I saw many other people walking with their hands held out like this.' She held her arms out in front of her, fingers extended. It was less painful to hold burned arms and hands horizontally than vertically, when the blood flowed down faster and became congested in the raw flesh. She joined the shuffling crowd of bleeding, half-naked people moving away from the city centre. The next thing she remembers is reaching a garden outside a big hospital. 'I lay down on the grass. Then it started to hurt – my eyes – I couldn't see any more.' She lay there all night.

Masako, who was also thirteen in 1945, thinks she saw the plane that dropped the bomb. She was at work with a squad of schoolfriends clearing demolished houses when someone said, 'Look, there goes another one!' as a B29 droned overhead. A few seconds later there was a flash and she was hurled to the ground. 'When I came to it was pitch dark all around, and absolutely silent. It was an extremely eerie experience. I had no idea what had happened; then gradually I heard moans and cries, like "Help . . . Mother . . ." and at first that was a relief, because I had feared I was alone. I looked around and saw people in a terrible state, burned and bleeding; I didn't realise that I looked just the same.'

She laughed, as if her ignorance and surprise were part of some huge joke. Talking to the women about their experiences I was surprised by how often they laughed and how frequently a smile was on their faces as they spoke. I was aware that the polite smile and the nervous laugh, used as a mask for other feelings in all cultures, are more frequent defence mechanisms in Japan: they are social reflexes that help make tricky encounters manageable. Then I was told by a Japanese that to smile as you suffer pain, even as you die, was traditionally admired, even advocated, as a sign of courage and indomitability.

Masako, now a social worker in her fifties, has a brisk, naturally cheerful manner. Her hands are slightly scarred but on her face there is only a flat brownish mark visible on one cheek; she has fluffy hair, a round face with a receding chin, and wears bright red lipstick and green eyeshadow. 'It was strange, but I didn't feel any pain at that stage,' she said. She managed to get back to her school with her friends, where she collapsed. She lay there, unable to see, for two days, until some soldiers took her to a makeshift hospital at one of the army parade grounds. 'More than fear, or pain, I was determined not to die in that place,' she said fiercely. 'I willed myself not to die.'

She lay on a mat on the ground for another full day; at some point she heard the mother of one of her friends nearby and managed to ask her to tell her family where she was. At last her father came to find her and take her home. He later told neighbours that she was such a terrible sight that at first he could feel no joy at having finally found her. He hoped she was not really his daughter after all. 'My face was all swollen and black and my body too,' said Masako and then she laughed again. 'My father had brought a cart to take me home; when he tried to pick me up, he didn't know where he could possibly hold me.' She returned home on 8 August. 'It was seventy-two hours, but thinking about it now it seems like a moment. Perhaps it is providence that protects people from remembering. Seventy-two hours is a long time to be suffering.'

Michiyo was twenty in August 1945, one of the oldest of the group which was to go to America and the oldest of the women I met. She hardly looks fifty, let alone sixty; she is a tiny, delicate woman with fine features, now almost unmarked, an oval face accentuated by hair drawn back into a bun at the nape of her neck, a gentle, youthful manner and a soft, almost diffident voice. She was on her way to work, as a clerk in a railway office, hurrying along because she was a few minutes late. The flash and the blast knocked her down and the next thing she remembers is that she was trapped by rubble under the ruins of a house.

'I crawled out — I don't know how, because my body was badly burned as well as my hands and lower face. Luckily I was wearing a white hat pulled down low which had protected the upper part of my face. The thick scarf I had been wearing on my shoulders was missing; also I was barefoot, my clogs had disappeared. Most of my trousers were missing too.' She too found herself holding her hands out in front of her like a sleepwalker, and joining the lines of dazed, burned, tattered people moving slowly in search of help. She reached an army parade ground where she collapsed, unable to move further. 'I didn't know what to do. I felt very weak; I had skipped breakfast because I was late. Later I learned that if I had been on time I would probably have been killed; most of my colleagues were, including three of my close friends.' She remembers her terrible thirst, but little else; someone gave her a biscuit, but she could not swallow it. Someone — perhaps a colleague, she thinks — miraculously found a stretcher and she was taken to a makeshift shelter, where eventually late that night her mother found her.

2

Hiroshima Consumed

When one sets the personal recollections of these women in the context given by official records, statistics and reports, it is astonishing that any of them came out alive. All of them were within two kilometres of the hypocentre (the point where the bomb exploded on the ground). Within this radius every building was either burned out or levelled by the blast. Most of the people in this area were severely burned, not by flames but by thermal radiation. The temperatures produced by the explosion are difficult to comprehend. It is hard to picture a fireball with a radius of fifteen metres, reaching a temperature of 300,000°C and emitting heat waves which travel at 1,200 feet per second. According to one report, 'The burst point probably reached a temperature of several million degrees centigrade within one millionth of a second after the explosion ... Infra-red rays were emitted in vast amounts 0.2 to 0.3 seconds after the explosion.' It was these infra-red rays of staggering heat intensity that caused the thermal burns suffered by the victims.

One characteristic of the incredible blast of heat that burned people up to about 3.5 kilometres away was that it could be deflected by what seemed afterwards like random, arbitrary and flimsy protection. Hats and clothing, especially in light colours and natural materials, occasionally shielded to some extent people more than a kilometre from the explosion. Those who were under cover, or in the shadow of some solid object, were sometimes entirely or partially protected. Not surprisingly, the closer you were to the hypocentre and the less cover you had, the more badly you were burned.

Some idea of the impact of such heat on human bodies can be gained from photographs taken soon after the bombing. It is often hard to be certain which part of a body is shown; the flesh seems to have melted like wax. It is difficult to look at such pictures; it is easier, and as instructive, to look at photographs of objects, or some objects themselves, exhibited in the Hiroshima Peace Museum. Telegraph poles and tree trunks several kilometres away were charred black on the surfaces facing the blast. Roof tiles broke into blister-like bubbles. Glass and metal melted into misshapen lumps.

As well as intense heat, the population was exposed to the atomic bomb's invisible destructive power, radiation. At the time, although top scientists and physicians in Japan as well as America were aware that an atomic explosion would bombard its victims with gamma rays and neutrons, and that this massive irradiation could destroy or damage the molecular structure of the cells in the human body, ordinary people, including doctors, had little or no idea of what the results might be. The people closest to the hypocentre, who received the largest doses of radiation, either died instantly or, if they survived, had other terrible and obvious injuries; it was not until ten days or two weeks after the explosion, when people apparently quite unhurt began to be severely ill, that the peculiar new power of the bomb began to be widely acknowledged and feared. Meanwhile, when the first symptoms of radiation sickness appeared in Hiroshima, including fever, diarrhoea and vomiting, the medical authorities responded as if an epidemic of dysentery had started.

In many ways, then, the women whose stories I was hearing could be thought lucky. This distinction was to complicate their lives and emotions, as it did for all the survivors of the bomb, who commonly felt amazed and even guilty that they had lived when so many around them had died. All reputable sources agree that the statistics, gathered in nightmarish circumstances and laboriously pieced together and extrapolated later, cannot be precise; but one survey states that in the area where most of the girls happened to be at the time, between 1.5 and 2 kilometres from the hypocentre, 13,322 people were killed and 7,627 severely injured. The mortality rate was 83 per cent for those with no protection. However, a little closer in, within 1 kilometre of the hypocentre, 90-100 per cent of those exposed were dead within a week.

If these schoolgirls who survived the atomic explosion were fortunate to do so, it was still tragic that so many boys and girls in their early teens were near the city centre at all. When I put this point to survivors in Hiroshima, they gave a resigned shrug. It was war. Small children and primary school pupils were sent away whenever possible and, according to the records, by July 1945 some 23,500 of these children had been evacuated; of course many of them then lost all or part of their families in the bombing, and became part of the wretched group who drifted back to the city afterwards and became known as A-Bomb Orphans. But secondary school pupils were required to serve their country. They took it as a matter of course.

On 25 March 1945 the government had announced the formation of what it called the People's Volunteer Corps; all Japanese men and women over the age of thirteen and under sixty, with the exception of pregnant women and the sick, were to be mobilised to work on war production. When the expected invasion of Japan came, they were to take up any weapons available to resist the invaders. As weapons were by that stage of the war in short supply, bamboo spears were recommended. In Hiroshima, the older secondary school students tended to be deployed in semi-skilled jobs in factories or depots on the outskirts of the city; the twelve- and thirteen-year-olds, like the women I met, were sent into the centre in large groups to perform simple physical tasks, connected with civil defence preparations, such as clearing rubble to make fire-breaks and routes through the city's narrow streets for fire-engines and ambulances. A disproportionately large number of them, therefore, were working near the hypocentre in the open air; according to one account, at least six working parties, each consisting of more than two hundred young people, were wiped out instantly.

For younger schoolchildren, of course, Japan had been at war first with China, then America, for as long as they could remember, and they and their parents had been educated under an aggressively nationalistic and militaristic regime. No questioning of Japan's glorious destiny was tolerated; the idea of defeat was unthinkable.

In Tokyo I happened to meet a woman whose experience helped me to understand the background to the bombing. Hiroko Nakamoto was fifteen when the bomb fell; her home was destroyed, her stepmother and half-sister were killed and she was badly burned. She remembers very well the atmosphere among schoolchildren before and during the war. After Japan went to war with China in 1937, women would stand on street corners in Hiroshima making *senninbaris* – 'a thousand people's needles'. These were long strips of white cloth six inches wide to be covered with red stitches contributed by innumerable women passers-by, and then sent to soldiers as belts, symbols of the trust and pride of Japanese womanhood. She also remembers that in the late 1930s, when food shortages began and rice was

15

scarce, refreshments were forbidden on school picnics so that the fighting men should not go short; and in winter, the children were not allowed to wear their warm coats to school. 'By being cold we were reminded of the soldiers who were fighting for our country in northern China,' she wrote in her memoir, *My Japan 1930-1951*.

When Hiroko was eleven Japan attacked America at Pearl Harbor. 'One cold December morning I came to school early. A classmate said: "Do you know we have started a war with America?" I could not believe it was the truth. I felt my heart beating very fast. I did not know what to say.' Hiroko's family, like many in Hiroshima, had relatives and friends living in the United States; she knew that it was a huge, modern and powerful place where people went to study and make money. 'Could Japan really be at war with that country, so rich, so far away? There was no school that day, nor the next. We were told to stay at home and listen to the news on the radio ... The radio was a government monopoly and nothing was broadcast now but news of the war, with martial music in between news broadcasts. Listening, I felt as if my blood were on fire, my body burning. The radio addressed us children, saying we must work hard for our country and prepare for the future. We did not know exactly what was meant. But I felt very sober as I went back to finish my last few months in primary school.'

Since August 1945 the name of Hiroshima has, for the rest of the world, stood for only one thing: the world's first nuclear bombing. It is still difficult for outsiders to remember that the place had an existence apart from that event, that it had centuries of fairly uneventful history and traditions that had nothing to do with the war. Hiroshima was known as a pleasant, proud, if provincial, city on a beautiful stretch of coastline,

16

famous throughout Japan for its seafood. In the capital, Tokyo, the Hiroshima mentality stood for a relaxed, somewhat slow and easygoing approach to life. It is as if the whole history of Baltimore in the United States, or Bristol in England, were to be cancelled out and overlaid with the image of one appalling, annihilating modern disaster. When you say you have spent some time in Hiroshima, people's expressions change. The word alone seems to demand a special response, some respectful expression of concern or distress. Pleasurable associations do not exist.

Among the survivors I met I found many agreeable, nostalgic recollections of what their city had been like. Indeed one of the minor resentments I came to sense in them was precisely this post-bomb obliteration of Hiroshima's pre-war reputation. 'My beautiful Hiroshima,' one of them called it, 'a city of lush greenery and clear water . . .' The city has a fine site at the foot of a ring of dramatically shaped small mountains which protect it from the cold winds blowing from the north off the Japan Sea, northern China and Siberia. Hiroshima is mild in winter and hot in summer. It looks towards the Inland Sea, one of the loveliest seascapes in the world, where calm silvery waters are dotted with thousands of islands, some tiny and uninhabited with deserted white beaches, some with small fishing communities, others with sizeable towns. Many are curved and pointed, their sharp peaks fringed along the skyline with pine trees, exactly like a Hiroshige landscape. Just off shore from Hiroshima, a short boat-ride away to the island of Miyajima, is one of the most celebrated religious centres in Japan, the Shinto shrine. The shrine dates from the ninth century and floats on the water at high tide; it is built from wooden piles and platforms painted a striking orange-red, as is the Tori, or gateway, shaped like a Greek pi sign, that guards the seaward

17

entry a hundred yards out into the water. Although the shrine is still a religious centre, where families come to be blessed or seek favours from young priests in white robes, and where student monks are looked after by devout virgins, it has always attracted parties of pleasure-seeking Japanese and foreign tourists. They come for its romantic walks and vistas, forests and beaches, the large herds of tame deer, the innumerable small bars and restaurants specialising in oysters and squid, and the teashops making and selling small maple-leaf shaped cakes of sweet bean paste, which are eaten with green tea and taste like *marrons glacés*.

Hiroshima itself, before the war, had one fine old building near the centre, a sixteenth-century castle; but the citizens were proud not so much of venerable buildings as of the natural beauties and healthy atmosphere of their city, especially the 'seven rivers' (really the channels of the delta of one river, the Ota). Hiroshima was often described as resembling the palm of a hand, the fingers being the river's branches. The city smelled of the sea and signs everywhere offered boats for hire. People would go swimming and boating or cormorant-watching, and there were restaurants all along the waterfront. Parks and gardens covered the lower slopes of the mountains, thick with the bright green of young willows in early spring and fruit blossom in early summer. Many wide streets in Hiroshima were lined with huge old pine trees. Hiroko lived on such a street, where the branches formed a canopy so dense she could not see the sky.

There was, however, another side to the character of Hiroshima, which as the war progressed made its citizens increasingly nervous. By the end of the nineteenth century, after three hundred years of obscurity, Hiroshima had become a place of some national importance. Ujina, the city's port, was built in the

1880s, part of the dramatic opening up of Japan to the outside world. During the Sino-Japanese War of 1894-5 the Imperial government briefly moved to Hiroshima Castle and conducted the war from there, while soldiers and supplies were shipped south to the front from Ujina. Thereafter Hiroshima became, as one local account puts it, 'an increasingly important military centre, with an economy that was largely dependent on army and navy expenditures . . . by the time the Pacific War erupted, the city housed the Hiroshima Eleventh Regiment, an army transport headquarters, a quarantine station, and munitions and supplies depots, as well as a number of other important military installations. With a population of some four hundred thousand, it was the seventh largest city in the country.'

Given these circumstances, it seemed likely that Hiroshima would sooner or later be a target for American bombers. The first air-raids on the Japanese mainland took place in the autumn of 1944; yet, by the spring of 1945, after Tokyo, Kobe and Osaka had been repeatedly hit, Hiroshima was still untouched. People wondered why. Strange rumours began to circulate. It was said that because so many people in Hiroshima had relations or connections in the United States, the city would be spared; there was even a wild story that the President had a relative living in the city. At the end of April, a lone B29 bomber flew over the city soon after dawn and dropped its load in the business district. Several banks and offices were damaged, but because it was so early only eleven people were killed. Everyone assumed that a wave of bombings would follow. Nothing happened.

Meanwhile the city had filled up with more and more soldiers. By the beginning of May, the Second General Army, charged with the defence of western Japan in the event of an invasion, established its headquarters in the

Castle. Evacuations and fire precautions were stepped up. Rumours of invasion reached even the schoolchildren, among them Hiroko N., by now a fourth-year secondary school student working in a factory:

> Time went on and we knew the war was getting more intense. We could bear it because we were sure Japan was winning. Soon it would be over. Our radio broadcasts told us of the glorious victories of our armies and the defeats suffered by the Americans. We heard only good news of Japan. And we believed it. One day a college girl who also worked in the factory said, 'I don't believe we are being told the truth. I don't think the war is going well for Japan.' We hated her. She lied. Was she pro-Western? Should we report her? No loyal Japanese would say such things about our country. Thus it was a great shock to us when the newspapers and radio informed us that the war was moving closer and we Japanese must be prepared for a fight on our own territory, on our own mainland. We young girls could not believe what we heard. The history of our country went back more than two thousand years. In all that time Japan had never been invaded. We had been taught that it never could be. Our country was protected by the gods. We were confident we would win this war as we had all others, because we were the country of the gods ... We were sure the gods would send some miracle to protect us from the cruel Americans.

By June 1945 air-raid warnings were beginning to keep Hiroshima alert during the day and awake at night. B29s roared overhead, from their bases in the Pacific islands, dropping mines in the Inland Sea or heading for smaller cities than Hiroshima. People listened in fear to the stories of refugees from Tokyo and Osaka which told of the firestorms they had seen; but comforted themselves with the thought that Hiroshima was surrounded by water. Surely that would protect them when the time came?

On 30 June the nearby port of Kure, a few miles away along the bay, was bombed all night; the people of Hiroshima could hear the explosions and see the glow. Army engineers began to blast holes in nearby mountains in order to construct fortifications for the coming invasion. Citizens' work groups were instructed to collect pine needles and pile them in great mounds around these fortifications, the idea being that when the bombers came overhead they would set the pine needles ablaze, and the smoke would provide instant camouflage. As people grew more and more nervous, some took to spending the nights in air-raid shelters. Others tried to leave the city but were sent back by the army and told that every last man and woman would be needed to fight fires and repel invaders.

Still people half-believed the assault would never happen, that Hiroshima was somehow special. It was so beautiful, so famous for its waters, mountains, trees and oysters, so close to the wonderful Miyajima shrine, some said, that the Americans had already chosen it as the place where they would like to settle when they finally arrived. They would not bomb the place where they intended to build villas and live as conquerors.

Hiroshima could not know that although Kyoto, the old capital, had been taken off the list of possible targets for the atomic bombing, Hiroshima had not. It was true that Hiroshima was under special protection, but not because of its natural amenities. Early in July the order had gone out from Washington to the commanders in the Pacific that four cities, Hiroshima among them, were not to be bombed. They were being reserved for the new weapon.

'At night now we seldom slept,' writes Hiroko N. 'It was summer and very hot. At home our air-raid shelter was stifling and full of mosquitoes that bit us mercilessly. Nights were spent sitting in the airless dark, slapping mosquitoes, listening to the sound of planes above us. With the factory, the August heat and the air-raids at night I, like almost everyone else in Hiroshima, was tired, very tired, all the time.'

3

After the Bombing

Neither the fire-breaks, nor the pine needles, nor the many rivers of Hiroshima provided any protection for the schoolchildren or the others beneath the bomb when it came. Within moments, fires broke out among the ruins and many people too weak to move were burned alive. The parks and river-banks began to fill with shocked and severely injured people. Some jumped into the water in their fear and pain, and many died there. Soon the rivers were dotted with bloated corpses. Everywhere there was a terrible, unforgettable smell.

Theoretically, Hiroshima had made efficient preparations for air raids; there were military police, civil defence teams and neighbourhood associations trained in firefighting and rescue techniques, and designated evacuation routes and centres. In the event none of these plans could be carried out. Civil administration had virtually broken down. The injured naturally tried to seek medical aid at hospitals and clinics; but most had been destroyed, and 90 per cent of the city's doctors and nurses had themselves been killed or injured.

People's next instinct was to make for home and find their families. It took a while for them to understand how complete the destruction was, and that there would be no houses left for them to shelter in if these had been within the inner ring; and it was still harder to accept that the child they had sent off to school that morning had vanished without trace, or that the mother left tidying the house was found only as a charred lump of flesh. Most families had made plans for where they would meet if separated after a bombing; usually it was at a neighbourhood evacuation site, on one of the army's parade grounds or at a school playground. Many bewildered and wounded people made their way to these meeting points to wait or search.

All the women whose stories I heard came through that day and the weeks and months that followed, when many who were in the same state died, because sooner or later they managed to make contact with a relative able to take care of them. Medical and emergency services were chaotic and minimal for many weeks. If your family could not look after you, your chances were poor. Many children died alone and untended.

Those who were able to care for the victims found their wounds unlike any they had seen before. The burns received by survivors who, like the girls, had been between 1.5 and just over 2 kilometres from the hypocentre, were technically entitled 'primary atomic bomb thermal injuries', or 'flash burns', caused by the direct action of heat rays upon the human body. It is likely, although none of them seems to have been aware of any protection, that all the group were in fact partly shielded from the thermal rays, since studies of burned survivors show that for those located as they were the mortality rate was about 70 per cent.

The main characteristic of severe flash burns is that the outer layer of skin is instantly destroyed. According to Dr Tomin Harada, who as a young doctor treated many Hiroshima burn victims soon after the end of the war, anyone exposed to the bomb at about 1.5 kilometres would receive third-degree burns, caused by the skin's exposure to heat of about 800°C for 0.6 of a second. 'An iron heated red hot and pressed against the skin would be about as hot,' he has said. 'The outer skin, the epithelium, is peeled off, instantly exposing the next layer of grey skin. After ten days this skin turns black and after three weeks it begins to crumble away, leaving bare flesh exposed. By that time flies have laid eggs on the wound and maggots are swarming in it. Foul-smelling pus is soiling the patient's bedding. After about two months the wound begins to decrease in size, but only very slowly. After about six months the festering stops and the wound closes.'

Most of the burn wounds suppurated or festered. This was partly because proper treatment was not available, conditions were unhygienic and the sufferers, often debilitated by a poor wartime diet, were not fed enough nourishing food. In addition, the effect of the radiation they had all received seemed to the doctors who saw the wounds in the early stages to complicate the healing process and lead to more unpleasant and prolonged infection. Most of the women I spoke to mentioned that their wounds were for a long time full of pus and painfully inflamed.

When after months of this misery the burns healed over and scar tissue formed, the scars too were different and were known by a special name. A keloid scar means a scar of a particularly thick, prominent nature that stands out from the body like a growth. The name was invented, Dr Harada told me, by Hippocrates and comes from the Greek word for crab claws, because the scars were thought to resemble crabs with claws extended. It was not, and still is not, known precisely what causes their appearance, but there appears to be a genetic predisposition in some non-European races to form keloids, especially after serious burns complicated by infection and undernourishment. Although no one has ever claimed that keloids originated with the bomb, there was a dramatic increase in their prevalence and seriousness among Hiroshima survivors, and during the first years after the bomb they became a dramatic and hated symbol of the experience.

Nearly all the women whose stories I traced were particularly unfortunate in that their keloid scars were very long lasting. As early as December 1946 it was apparent that younger people were especially likely to develop keloids; 80 or 90 per cent of those exposed to the bomb within a radius of 2 kilometres had keloids by the end of 1945. However, as time passed, many scars dwindled and even virtually disappeared; they were at their worst about three months after the bombing, but six months later showed a remarkable decline. Over the next ten years, they continued to become gradually less prevalent and serious. A long-term study between 1946 and 1956 showed a relatively rapid decrease in size of keloids after the peak in 1946-7. Frequently the keloids shrank into ordinary scars. At the time, however, no one knew how long the scars were likely to last; all that the scarred girls knew was that their keloids attracted attention every time they went out, and that they could not be sure that they would ever disappear.

For Terue, whose father had hardly recognised her when she reached him, standing bleeding in the ruins of their house, it was her father's devotion that made all the difference. He had been in the army and had a little medical knowledge; he found a can of car oil in the debris and smeared her with it, which she believes was the right thing to do and helped her burns to heal eventually. 'After that the treatment I got was very primitive,' she said. 'My father was cut all over by splinters of glass but he managed to carry me and to lead my younger brother, who was unhurt, to the East Parade Ground. There was a doctor there but all he had was some mercurochrome. I was in great pain; my father did everything he could think of to alleviate it . . .

26

There were some cucumbers and potatoes growing nearby and people believed that cucumber was especially soothing for burns, as it cooled them.' After a week or so her father managed to move them out to his home village; a school had been turned into an emergency shelter for bomb victims. There, Terue remembers, her burns were dressed; each time the dressings were changed it was like peeling away another layer of skin.

That summer was very hot; flies swarmed everywhere. 'The most important part of the treatment was to prevent festering,' said Terue calmly. 'Many people were black with flies, and the flies laid eggs in their wounds. I was lucky; my father was so careful that not one maggot was able to breed on me. Most people were covered with them.'

It took nearly a year, she recalls, for her burns to heal. In the meantime, all her hair fell out; this was one of the signs of the mysterious new sickness caused by radiation, which the people of Hiroshima were by now calling A-Bomb Disease. Most of the women I met had a bout of this illness, but recovered. 'I was very afraid my hair would not grow back,' said Terue. 'I had to wear a scarf all the time.' As her sight gradually improved she could see the burn scars on her hands and legs; she began to be very anxious about what her face looked like. When she tried to find a mirror, she discovered that her father had removed them all.

She could feel with her fingers that her face had changed. The entire left side of her face was distorted: her left eye would not close and wept continuously, her left eyebrow was half gone, her mouth was pulled up at the corner. Worst of all, she developed large lumpy keloid scars on her limbs and face. They stood out grotesquely; they were sensitive to the touch and sometimes acutely irritating or painful. In cold weather, they went a bluish purple; in the heat they went dark red. 'I

27

had one here that was more prominent than my nose,' said Terue, touching her left cheekbone. 'And I also developed a huge keloid on the back of my hand.'

Terue's father was convinced that constant massaging and manipulating of keloid scars would help to make them smaller, perhaps even get rid of them in time. He also believed that by exercising her scarred hand and her distorted left elbow, she would regain flexibility and prevent her limbs from freezing into a cramped, distorted position. He made his daughter rub and knead her keloids. 'I had to massage the scars for hours every day, three hundred and sixty-five days a year,' said Terue. 'Sometimes they would bleed; it was often very painful. If I stopped too soon, or tried to miss a day, my father would get very angry; he was even prepared to hit me to force me to continue.' She thought at the time he was being too hard on her; they had some furious battles. 'Now, I feel very thankful to my father. When I saw the other girls who went to America, their faces were worse then mine. Most of them had crooked, frozen fingers. Mine were straight.'

Although her scars gradually seemed to get a little better, and her hair grew back, Terue was miserably self-conscious about her appearance, especially about her staring, weeping left eye. She wore a patch over it, but she still hated going out of doors. 'It required a lot of courage to leave the house at all,' she said. 'Again it was my father who made me go out, for my own good.' All the same, she spent a lot of time at home alone.

Michiko Y., another thirteen-year-old, whose mother pulled her out from beneath a collapsed wall near their house, dragged herself to Hijiyama Park while her mother went back to look for her ten-year-old cousin. The boy had vanished on his way to school; his body was never found. Their house had been burned down.

When her mother found Michiko in the park she was unconscious; she revived her, and they were both advised by a soldier to try to get out of the city. When they reached the port of Ujina, the wounded were being herded on to boats which would take them to refugee centres or emergency clinics on nearby islands like Ninoshima, or to ports around the bay outside the devastated area. Michiko, still in a semi-conscious state, spent a night with her mother in a fishing village; the next day they were ordered on to another boat, which left them on a sandy beach between Hiroshima and Kure.

There, hardly able to see, Michiko lay for weeks on the floor of a reed hut built for pre-war summer swimming parties. She heard a soldier swear at her mother for pestering him to give her daughter something for her pain; and she remembers the constant swish of the fan her mother used to keep the flies away. She can also recall hearing the voice of the Emperor addressing the nation on 15 August — nine days after the bombing of Hiroshima and six days after a second atomic bomb was dropped, on Nagasaki — announcing the capitulation of Japan. It was the first time his subjects had ever heard his voice.

Michiko and her mother had lived alone before the war; with no relatives in Hiroshima and no house, they stayed on in the beach hut after nearly all the others had left. In late September the weather in those parts becomes stormy; that year, to add to the people's miseries, a typhoon struck on 17 September. The local fire brigade came to persuade the last refugees to leave; Michiko and her mother refused. They had nowhere to go. 'I remember praying that I would die,' said Michiko. 'Mother and I would listen to the wind and the rain at night and weep, and wonder what we had done to deserve what was happening to us.' Finally, as winter approached, the authorities insisted that the hut be closed. The handful of people still at the beach were taken to a primary school near the city. 'There were several lotus ponds near the school,' said Michiko. 'Almost all we had to eat was lotus roots dipped in salt.'

When eventually they made their way back into the city, they built themselves a shack in the ruins near where their small house had been. They raised the money from the sale of the kimonos that were to have been Michiko's trousseau, which her mother had sent for safe-keeping to relatives in the country. They bought a sewing machine and scraped a living as dressmakers. Every night Michiko's mother rubbed her keloids with cream or oil, when they could afford it. Gradually the scars improved, but her head was pulled down to one side as the skin contracted and her mouth and eye were pulled out of shape. 'When I met former friends in the street,' said Michiko, 'I would see a surprised look on their faces. One friend said to me, "Oh, I didn't realise you were alive." '

4

'A New, Ugly Me'

As the girls recovered, sooner or later they realised that their appearance had been permanently changed. For many of them, the occasion when they first saw themselves in a mirror and understood how badly damaged their faces were has remained a frozen moment, distinct and still acutely painful. As I went about Hiroshima, my eyes were often drawn to groups of Japanese schoolgirls in their early teens, with smooth curved cheeks, delicate necks and thick, swinging, blue-black hair, giggling and whispering and glancing at themselves in the windows of trams and shops. There are lumpy and spotty teenage skins in Japan as elsewhere, but the girls I saw seemed all to have the very best complexions. Even middle-aged Japanese women have smoother, tauter skin than most Westerners, and the unblemished skin on the faces of the women in the group was always fine and youthful-looking. At night, when I rubbed in my own face cream, I would wonder how it must be to feel the change from skin texture to scar tissue, and would for an instant experience a minute tremor of the shock and pain these women could recall so clearly.

One girl, Yukiko, wrote an account of how she discovered what had happened to her, quoted by Kazuo Chujo.

> I was lying in bed. There was a glass bottle nearby. The room was dark near the ceiling, so that the bottle's glass surface acted as a mirror. What I saw there was the most

31

ghastly image I'd ever seen in my life. 'Please, no, this can't be my face?' For some moments I was numb with shock. Then a tear fell from one of my staring eyes. Then another. More. Tears came flooding out. I sobbed uncontrollably.

When I got well enough to leave bed, I began to go stealthily to my dressing-table. I tried to get used to my face. The original body given me by my mother had simply ceased to exist. In its place was a new, ugly me born of the atomic bomb. It was this new me I had to encounter . . . There were times when I simply could not be thankful to be alive or feel grateful to those who were nursing me. I envied the dead. You can't imagine what a terrible burden it was to keep living. I was only a young girl, just entering that period in life which should normally be filled with rosy dreams and carefree laughter. It was as if I had been condemned to a life of bitter weeping. There was absolutely nothing I could hope for in life. Death became the only thing I could think of day and night.

Another very badly burned girl, Hiroko T., caught sight of herself in the bowl of a spoon. 'I was in bed for months after the bombing,' she said. 'I knew I was badly hurt but I didn't think too much about my face. One day I was eating soup, in bed, and I saw myself; that was when I found out something was really wrong.' Her mouth and chin were almost obliterated by massive red scars, and her chin was pulled in to her neck, which was also a mass of twisted, lumpy scarring. Nevertheless she went back to school, and remembers telling herself that she must try to feel proud of her scars, that like a soldier she had been wounded on behalf of her country. Her father had been killed in the war two years before the bombing.

It was only when she first went to work, as a clerk in a small local government office on an island in the Inland Sea, that she really became aware of people's reactions to her injuries. She was nicknamed 'Red Monster' and took to wearing a mask over the lower part of her face.

Shigeko too has vivid recollections of how she learned about her face.

I knew I had hurt my face but I didn't know what I looked like. The mirrors were all gone. One day, accidentally, I saw the reflection of my face in a piece of glass on the ground. I couldn't believe it was my face. I looked carefully [she imitated a puzzled frown and intent stare] and I felt shock, like when someone drops ice-cold water down your back and makes you shiver, or when someone jumps out at you in the dark [she started violently]. My face like *this*? I didn't cry out or scream, no noise, but the tears ran like hot water, burning all down my face.

My mother and sister said, 'You'll be OK, you'll be OK: it's still the healing process.' I believed it for a long, long time, that a normal face would come back. But I still looked horrible; my eyebrows had not grown back and my whole face was pink. When I went outside the children said to me, 'Hello Hello, give me chewing gum!' There were many American soldiers around in those days and they thought I had become American because of my pink face and big eyes. Now everyone is used to American faces, but not then.

I didn't go back to school because after it burned they moved it outside the city and my mother was afraid I couldn't hang on to the train — which was always very crowded — because of my burned hands. We didn't know the bomb was called the atomic bomb, so we called it Pikadon — 'pik' means flash and 'don' a big noise. So children would call after anyone with burns — 'Pikadon, there goes the Pikadon!' It upset me, yes; but I just ran away, I didn't want to fight over it. My sister wanted to fight, she didn't like it. And later on, when many new people came to live in the city after the war, who didn't know about the bombing, when I went out people would go 'AAAGH' and look at me, and say, 'What happened to her . . .?' These things I *hated*. I said, 'Let's go home.' My sister said, 'Don't stare at her, it could have happened to you' . . . Now I'm not shy, I'm outspoken, but in those days I was very shy, I hated arguments, I cried instead.

My aunts and neighbours, who knew me before I was burned, they were always saying, 'Poor Shigeko, if only she hadn't been burned, she was such a pretty girl.' That helped, that really supported me, that I once had a pretty face.

Many people, of course, were badly scarred in post-war Hiroshima. It is estimated that about 100,000 people were burned or otherwise injured, but survived; the schoolgirls and young women I was concerned with were a tiny, atypical group who were at least fortunate enough to be nursed back to health, and to recover sufficiently within the first year to be able to walk and even in some cases go back to school. Several of them said to me that for a while after the bombing they felt in no way exceptional; they could see that a great many people were as badly off or worse off than themselves, and the problems of survival for ordinary families – how to rebuild or build a house, earn money, get enough to eat – were so acute that the longer-term problems of adjusting to life with a damaged face took some time to develop.

Soon after the bombing, there were rumours that the soil and atmosphere of Hiroshima had been so poisoned by the mysterious new weapon that nothing would grow there for seventy-five years. But by early in 1946 it was apparent that this was not so. On the contrary, a startlingly vigorous regeneration seemed to be taking place. Sometimes this was alarming, as when plants grew to several times their normal size and strange weeds proliferated wildly over the charred ruins; but sometimes it was a sign of hope, as when two blackened stumps of cherry trees near the old Town Hall broke into blossom the following spring.

Human activity too was vigorous and unexpected. Far from abandoning the centre of the city, within weeks people were moving back, putting up shacks either on their property or someone else's. Squatters were left alone. Refugees and returning evacuees streamed into the city. When the Occupation forces arrived, the people of Hiroshima found that the Australian and American soldiers were not the raping, looting monsters they had feared but generally well-disciplined, often genial men who gave the children chewing gum. The Americans found much less hostility from the citizens than they had expected: some felt that Japanese fatalism and respect for authority contributed to this acceptance of the Occupation. Like any garrison town, Hiroshima had developed a flourishing red-light and entertainments district; it was not long before it sprang up again, under bosses anxious to cater for the needs of the Occupation soldiers. A black market began to operate, centred around the ruined station, together with pinball parlours often run by a tough new post-war breed of Americanised gangster.

Along with a resurgent vitality there was a dark side to the rapid re-establishment of urban life in Hiroshima. Ambivalent, even hostile feelings emerged towards people who were visibly damaged by the atomic explosion. As the new Hiroshima developed, the survivors, especially those badly scarred, began to feel discriminated against and despised. It was suggested to me in Japan that this discrimination was in part due to the religious and cultural traditions of the country, whereby people who are in any way different or handicapped are feared and avoided. In Japan, I was told, most people's embarrassment at disability or deformity is so strong that their response, confronted by a person in difficulty, is to ignore them. Japan for a long time lagged behind other countries in provisions for the disabled.

There is even, apparently, a basis in Buddhism for ignoring or disregarding the problems of the crippled or disfigured; one's fate is pre-ordained, it is pointless to fight it. I also encountered the lingering and, in the context of the bombing of Hiroshima, inexplicable idea that such a terrible fate must indicate divine retribution for bad actions, that anyone who suffered the bombing must somehow have deserved it.

More specifically, it became apparent that the *hibakusha*, as they were called (literally, explosion-affected people), were often regarded by others as tainted. The continuing mysteriousness of delayed physical symptoms caused by the bombing, the various forms of sickness evidently somehow related to it, ranging from acute illnesses to demoralising, general feelings of exhaustion and anaemia, made people afraid of physical contact with survivors. Whether through discretion or good fortune, none of the women I spoke to mentioned particular instances of being publicly shunned, although their awareness of being forced to live restricted lives was clear enough. The literature of *hibakusha* experience is full of examples. Public baths, a popular institution all over Japan, refused entry to men and women with keloids in case they contaminated the water. A young woman with an injured leg who went to work in a pinball parlour told an interviewer:

All the other girls who had to work there dreaded the daylight, either because the debt collectors were after them or because they had such hideous burn scars as a result of the Pikadon that they could only hope to get the sort of job where no one ever saw their faces . . . Those girls whose bodies were scarred by a keloid . . . were not even allowed to hang their laundry up to dry near the other girls' clothes,

36

and the plates off which they ate were kept away from the rest and were washed up separately.

Even among *hibakusha* themselves, those with keloids were avoided. A young man told the American psychiatrist Robert Jay Lifton:

> Of all the things connected with those days, what makes the strongest impression on me is the mark of a burn scar . . . I really hate to see a keloid . . . when I do, rather than sympathy, the strongest feeling I have is to try to avoid seeing it . . . When I see a keloid on a young girl she seems to have become a deformed person . . . and I think that anyone finds it painful to look at a deformed person.

Against this background, it is hardly surprising that most of the injured girls withdrew into themselves, stayed at home much of the time and sank into depression. One of the most painful results of their experience must have been the realisation that their chances of marrying were badly reduced. Most marriages in Japan were arranged by matchmakers, who usually declined to help *hibakusha*. Even today in Japan, and more than in most advanced societies, marriage is regarded as every girl's purpose in life; qualified women graduates still mostly assume that they will marry and give up work well before they are thirty. These girls were not highly educated; they mostly came from modest, traditional, provincial Japanese homes. It was terrible for them to know that not only did their damaged faces and bodies make them unattractive to men, but that there were strong rumours that the bomb had affected the fertility of female victims and their capacity to bear normal children. I found it hard to question the women I met about this subject; the Japanese hate discussing personal matters, but the women I spoke to did their best.

Toyoko, one of the eldest of the group, was nineteen when she was injured. Whereas the younger girls had presumably not had time to think much about romance or marriage before they were hurt, I imagined she perhaps had done so. Without specifically stating as much, she did convey to me the strong impression that she had never stopped feeling anger and sadness at the effect her facial injuries have had on her relationships with men and her chances of marriage.

She is still one of the most disfigured of the women, and in her twenties, before plastic surgery, her face must have been dramatically distorted. 'I had trouble with my mouth,' she told me, putting her hand to her lips, which are still a little twisted. 'I couldn't open it very wide . . . and also my neck, I couldn't move it properly.' Keloids then covered much of her lower face. 'The colour was very red, so you see . . . I didn't like to go out. Now we have good make-up, but then there was not much, just powder, and anyway not many girls wore much. Now everyone wears make-up if they want to and it is much easier.'

Had she found it hard, after the war, to make friends with young men? 'Oh yes,' she said, smiling ruefully and looking at me as if the answer to my question was obvious enough. 'I was nineteen years old, so you see . . . Maybe I didn't look like a proper woman, but my feelings inside had not changed.' She tried to explain, in halting English, that she felt a kind of rage that because her face had been damaged she was expected to be grateful if any man paid attention to her. 'If I don't like a man, I don't want him. Even if I have bad scars . . . Even if a man propose to me, it's difficult to believe if it's true, or maybe not? I don't have very high ideals, but I have some ideals, you see? Inside I have the same hopes, same dreams! It's difficult to change. Maybe that's why I'm single. Many of the girls like me are single, you see.' Had she then always assumed that she would marry and have children? Again, she smiled. 'This is not our hoping, to be single,' she said.

Michiyo, another girl who had already reached an age when she might have expected to marry, seemed more resigned to her single life, although as she spoke of her feelings a look of wistfulness came over her small face with its flat, pale-brown scar. After the war she had very bad keloids on her throat, her breasts and back, but they gradually disappeared without treatment and her main lingering problem was a badly scarred and stiffened left arm. 'I could not bend it,' she said, holding it out rigidly to show me. 'If I tried, and forced it to bend, it would get stuck, and the wounds would open and bleed. Keloids had formed on it. It looked like a chicken's leg.' She told me that she used to dream that her arm became magically better; but at least her worst scar was not on her face. 'I considered myself very lucky.'

All the same she was embarrassed by her useless arm and tried to avoid situations where it would be noticed; instead of trying to find another office job, she decided to stay at home and teach the traditional skills of well brought-up Japanese women — flower arranging and the tea ceremony. For these she would wear long-sleeved kimonos to conceal her arm from strangers. She also, she says, gave up the idea of marriage. 'I just didn't feel very sociable . . . and marriage, then, was not just a matter of meeting a boyfriend. There had to be introductions and formal arrangements.' But had she assumed, before she was injured, that one day she would be married and have children? Michiyo managed to convey, even through an interpreter, the polite but determined resistance of the Japanese woman to pressing personal questions. 'Maybe in a general way I might have thought of it. I also thought — though perhaps I was trying to convince myself — that marriage is not the ultimate guarantee of happiness anyway. And at that time, there were so many women compared to men, that for most of us, unless there was a man wanting very much to marry us and we too were very much in love, it was better not to think about it.' She smiled and added: 'It is not that we were happy about the situation; we all had some hopes, once. But we grew older, and they faded.'

Shigeko, who cherished the knowledge that she had once been considered pretty, thinks now that she made a deliberate attempt, as a teenager, to put thoughts of love and marriage out of her head. 'I didn't want to be a cry-baby,' she said fiercely. 'After the bomb, I said to myself, "I'm going to love everybody the same way, so I don't have to worry . . ." ' Like Michiyo, she reminded me that in those days courtship and marriage in Japan were usually arranged and always discreet and formal matters, not casual and open as they are increasingly today. 'If a girl had a boyfriend, it was sort of a secret,' she said. 'That helped me, too.' She had a close girlfriend who, she said, once hurt her feelings more than any boy ever did. 'She promised to go to a movie with me and she didn't show up; then I found out that she went with a boy and didn't tell me. *That* hurt me!' She learned another lesson when her sister married, through the offices of a matchmaker. 'When the matchmaker was coming to the house, normally, she would have asked if she could look after me too. But when she saw me, she just said, "Oh, I see — goodbye," and went home. That taught me. So I said to myself, "A bomb destroyed my face, so I have an ugly face. It's normal that disfigured people never get married." But still, I was a young girl, and I'd look at good-looking boys passing by and think, "How nice." ' She laughed with genuine merriment at the thought of her teenage susceptibility.

5

Seeking Help

During the late 1940s, under the American Occupation of Japan, there were no co-ordinated attempts to help atomic bomb victims and no free treatment. Indeed, during the Occupation all information on and research into their plight were severely restricted under the Press Code issued by American Headquarters in September 1945. 'At the first meeting of the Special Committee for the Investigation of A-Bomb Damages,' says one official account, 'the person in charge of the GHQ's Economic and Scientific Bureau served notice that further surveys and study of A-Bomb matters by the Japanese would require permission from GHQ and publication of A-Bomb data was thenceforth prohibited.' Official policy was to suppress and play down all accounts of atomic bomb damage. In October 1945, a Japanese film team making a documentary record in Hiroshima and Nagasaki was arrested; in December, all film footage was confiscated and turned over to the US Strategic Bombing Survey Team. All further reporting, filming and photography by the Japanese was forbidden.

Efforts by the victims themselves to ask for help were not encouraged. In 1948 a woman working for the Ministry of Labour made a survey of the needs of female A-Bomb victims; her report was suppressed. A group of women in Hiroshima then held a meeting which drafted an appeal to the Japanese Prime Minister to provide medical care and relief measures for survivors. This appeal is now recognised as the first statement of

41

victims' needs and aspirations, but at the time it was ignored.

Despite the restrictions, a certain amount of information about the horrors of the bombings and their after-effects did emerge; often through foreign reporters. The most effective was an American, John Hersey, who reported from Hiroshima for the *New Yorker* in the summer of 1946. For the first time the American public was compelled to relate the use of the bomb to the sufferings of individuals.

In 1952 the American Occupation came to an end and censorship of information about the atomic bombings was lifted. The details that began to emerge shook the consciences of other Japanese and of some Americans. In 1952 a leading Tokyo news magazine published a special supplement of pictures taken shortly after the bombings; this was the first time a mass readership had seen such pictures. Japanese reporters began to visit the bombed cities and write their own stories; the young people with terrible scars, especially the girls and young women, who came to be known as A-Bomb Maidens, Keloid Girls or Hiroshima Maidens, caught the public attention, and attempts to organise treatment for them began.

The ending of the Occupation also allowed the curious position of the main American medical organisation in Hiroshima to be examined and criticised. Since 1947, the Atomic Bomb Casualty Commission had been investigating the effects of the bomb. Among the problems to which they were directed by a preliminary survey carried out by American scientists were: cancer, leukaemia, shortening of life, loss of vigour, growth and developmental disorders, sterility and genetic alteration. By 1950 the Atomic Bomb Casualty Commission was a huge operation based in an imposing new white building overlooking the city. Teams of researchers organised regular visits by bomb victims; but although they were examined and diagnosed and monitored, they were not given any treatment. This, not surprisingly, made the researchers widely disliked and resented.

There were various other reasons, I discovered, why little was done during the first five or six years after the bombing to repair the scarred faces of the survivors. At first such injuries, though ugly and painful, seemed comparatively superficial. When it became apparent that keloids did sometimes shrink spontaneously, the need to operate seemed to diminish. But above all surgeons were reluctant to cut away the scars and attempt skin grafts because in cases undertaken early on, the keloids recurred as badly as before: occasionally, operating seemed to make them worse. In December 1945 a leading dermatologist at Hiroshima's Red Cross Hospital warned that premature surgery might be dangerous. The treatment he recommended included ointments, massage and visits to hot springs; it was also important, he said, that the victims should have plenty of rest and a good nourishing diet, neither of which was easy to come by in post-war Hiroshima.

By early 1947, Dr Masao Tsuzuki, Japan's leading expert in atomic bomb injuries, announced that in his view the growth period for radiation-induced keloids had passed and surgical removal could be recommended; but even then surgeons remained reluctant, especially where the main aim was to improve the face. Keloid-distorted feet, arms and legs were more urgent; and, besides, plastic or reconstructive surgery was not much practised in Japan.

Dr Tomin Harada, one of the first plastic surgeons in Japan and a man who played an important part in the lives of the women in the group, still works as a surgeon in Hiroshima. He is now in his early seventies, a tall, kindly-looking man who lives in a pleasant modern house a little way out of central Hiroshima.

'In Japan, plastic surgery used to be ranked very low,' he said. 'Most physicians looked on it as not so respectable. In Oriental thinking, the body you were born with should not be changed. It was also believed that ugliness came from inside, and that only if the spirit is good do the features show beautifulness.' Most people trying to improve their appearance in pre-war Japan were not respected – especially, Dr Harada reminded me, because often what they wanted was cosmetic operations on their eyelids and noses to make them more fashionably European. This disapproval of plastic surgery made treatment for scarred bomb victims a still more remote possibility.

Dr Harada, who was born into a prosperous middle-class family in Hiroshima in 1912 and studied medicine in Tokyo, became interested in skin grafting while working in the surgical department at medical school. 'When I graduated in 1936 this science was primitive,' he said. 'There were no books on the subject in Japan, and no description of methods. I devised a method myself and had some success in a few cases.' Plastic surgery, he told me, had really only been established as a modern surgical speciality in England, after the First World War, when the British surgeon Harold Gillies published his book *Plastic Surgery of the Face*. However, Dr Harada's first skin graft, which he performed as a favour on a nephew who had hurt his leg skiing and lost a lot of skin, was based on an American method he had read about, called a pinch graft. Small pieces of skin are pinched up with forceps, and then snipped off and laid over the wound. 'Within three weeks the wound was completely healed,' he later wrote. 'That was quite an achievement for that time and I was very pleased with the success; but since such examples were extremely rare, the university surgeons did not follow it up.'

In 1938 Dr Harada was drafted into the army. He spent the next eight years as an army surgeon in China. 'I was eager to go, but at the same time I had little military spirit,' he wrote. 'I considered war unfortunate, but I did not yet consider it a crime or something that should be stopped. I did not accept the ideology that said that Japan should lead the world, but was extremely critical of the colonialism of Britain, the United States and Holland.' When the atomic bombs were dropped on Hiroshima and Nagasaki Dr Harada was stationed on Taiwan, as head of a medical unit. He heard what had happened to his home town, where his wife and young children were living, when the announcement of Japan's surrender came on 15 August; that night, he wrote later, he had a dream. He seemed to see Hiroshima laid waste, full of blackened corpses; he went back to the hospital where he had worked, but found only ruins.

'Then I saw a long line of people. All were naked. Their skin had peeled off and there was no hair on their heads. There was one doctor. He seemed to be using something like a paint brush to paint them with mercurochrome. "That is no good! You must graft on skin!" I found myself shouting . . .' He woke up convinced that he should dedicate his life to helping the injured of Hiroshima. 'I supposed there must be a need for plastic surgery because of the atomic bombings,' he says now. 'I decided that if I got back to Hiroshima, I would do my best.'

When he returned in May 1946 he found to his joy that his wife and family were safe, having left the city before the bombing to stay with relatives. Their home in the centre had been completely destroyed. He was advised to stay in the suburbs, but decided to build a small hospital on the site of the old one where he had worked before the war. 'In autumn 1946 I constructed a small wooden hospital, like a barracks, in the centre of

45

the city. Gradually patients came back; there were many scarred people. About 80 per cent of burned patients developed keloids.'

Dr Harada became one of Japan's foremost experts on keloids. 'In my experience,' he said, 'white people do not often develop keloids. Negroes often do; the Japanese are in between. In the bombing, there were very few keloids among people exposed within a radius of 1 kilometre from the hypocentre; they were mostly dead. The 10 per cent who survived were very ill for two or three years; their vitality was very low, so keloids did not grow. Most keloids appeared on people exposed within a radius of 1.5 to 2 kilometres. The highest incidence of keloids was at 1.8 kilometres. If the exposed parts of the body were small in area, there was a low incidence. If the burned surface covered 30 to 40 per cent of the body, the patients mostly died. With 15 to 20 per cent body exposure there was a high incidence of keloids. Another factor was healing time. If the burns healed quickly, within one month, the keloids were not so big. The worst took between two and four months. And there was also the age factor. Older people seldom produced keloids, and neither did the very young. Those aged between ten and twenty-five had the highest incidence of keloids.'

I asked Dr Harada whether scars from thermal burns caused by radiation were different from other scars. 'Among Japanese, ordinary burns produce keloid scars in maybe 20 per cent of cases, but the thickening of the skin is not so great. I suppose radiation played a part; those exposed to it in the middle range of severity displayed very pronounced keloids.' So radiation was an important cause of keloids, in his view? 'Very few scientists have studied such keloids; there has been no opportunity,' he replied cautiously. 'From my observations, the excessive scar tissues were produced by the body's immune reaction to radiation.'

Regarding cases of spontaneous disappearance of keloids, he had observed that for about four years after the bombing the scars were at their worst: within five to ten years, a significant proportion of them went away. All the same, people frequently needed treatment for keloids: 'Sometimes they were very painful, or they would itch unbearably; people could not sleep.'

Sometimes the keloids were not just ugly, they were crippling; one of Dr Harada's early cases was a small boy who was being carried on his mother's back when the bomb's thermal rays caught them. Her face and the boy's legs from knees to toes were horribly burned. The keloids on his ankles pulled his feet back into a 'V' shape; he could only walk on his heels, and then just for a few painful steps. He could not wear shoes and so seldom went outside; his mother was uncertain whether he could manage to start school. Dr Harada carried out a successful skin graft in his case, but was not so successful with others. 'In 1947 and 1948 I made some experiments with skin grafts,' he said. 'Initially they were successful but after three months the grafts were destroyed by the recurrence of the keloids. Within five years, almost all the keloids removed recurred. After ten years, very few. It depended on the person; individual tendencies were very important. Most surgeons were afraid to undertake surgery on keloids for five or six years after the bombing; I did thirty or forty cases.'

By the early 1950s, then, circumstances affecting the treatment of survivors were beginning to change. Dr Harada had by this time seen and treated a number of scarred young women, some of whom were to be members of the Hiroshima Maidens project. One was Michiko S., who had been injured, like so many others, as a schoolgirl of thirteen. Dr Harada vividly remembers the occasion when she first came to see him, wearing a mask over her face, in 1953. At the time a famous American plastic surgeon, Professor Truman Blocker of the University of Texas, was visiting the Atomic Bomb Casualty Commission to examine bomb victims.

'I was involved in a program which was seeking to get government aid for survivors of the atomic bomb and so had arranged to be present when Dr Blocker examined patients,' wrote Dr Harada later. 'My first idea was to obtain medical insurance, so I was putting together an album of pictures of keloid victims to show the officials in the Welfare Ministry and members of the Diet [the Japanese legislature]. When Michiko removed her mask and I saw her face, I could hardly keep from gasping. I noticed that Dr Blocker also winced. When I explained to her why I wanted a picture and asked her permission, she said "Yes" with no expression whatever. But I had become so nervous that the color slide I took was not usable.'

Dr Harada got to know Michiko S. quite well and learned her story. She had been the captain of her class, which had been assigned to demolition clearance work 1.6 kilometres from the hypocentre. Her face was so badly burned that when she put her hands up to her face, her eyelids came away on her fingers. She tried to find help, but collapsed and lay semi-conscious for three days; she remembered hearing a soldier say, 'Look, here's another dead schoolgirl, think we should burn this one?' She felt sure, later, that many people were burned alive.

Both Michiko's parents had died years before, and she and her sisters were brought up by their grandmother. Eventually Michiko was taken home, and after three months or so with only minimal treatment she was able to get out of bed. The first time she saw her face she thought it hardly looked human at all. Dr Harada has reported what he saw, seven years later. 'I don't know how to describe her face. The entire surface was like some rough reddish earthenware. The nose was practically nonexistent except for two small holes ... The shrunken mouth was shut tight as if bolted. There were no eyebrows except for their distorted vestiges arching up improbably towards the brows. The eyelids folded outwards, making blinking an impossibility. The eyes constantly discharged a pus-like substance that streaked down her cheeks unless wiped away frequently.' As Michiko herself said, 'I'm sure he was shocked out of his wits. Who wouldn't be? I had a face so horrifying that even I myself couldn't look at it without feeling sick to my stomach.'

Both Dr Harada and Professor Blocker urged Michiko to have an operation on her eyelids as soon as possible; they feared she might otherwise lose her sight. She and her grandmother agreed. Dr Blocker performed the first operation. He took very thin skin from the inside of her thigh, and used it to give her new upper eyelids; Dr Harada did the same for her lower lids. 'A month after the first operation she left the hospital with both eyes improved,' he says. 'Now that her eyes could open and close normally, the external disfiguration which had seemed so frightful before the surgery had completely disappeared.'

Although Dr Harada hoped that Michiko would continue with plastic surgery to improve her appearance, she went home with her grandmother. At this time, all Japanese medical care had to be paid for, and many bomb victims were unable to afford it. Plastic surgery was especially expensive as it usually required a series of operations and long stays in hospital. It was still the custom in Japan for family members to stay in hospital with patients to help with nursing, and most people found it difficult financially to do so, even if they were able to take the time off from work.

At the centre of local attempts in the early 1950s to help the Hiroshima Maidens was a Japanese Christian minister, the Reverend Kiyoshi Tanimoto. He was one of the six people whose moment-by-moment experiences on 6 August 1945 formed the basis of John Hersey's account, and the publication of the story changed his life and the lives of a large number of other survivors, including the women in the group.

The Reverend Tanimoto no longer actively runs his parish, but he still lives in Hiroshima and plays a part in church activities. He is seventy-four now and has not been well; but when I went to talk to him in his small modern house on a hillside overlooking the Inland Sea he was still eager to help me by recalling the early days after the bombing. He is a slight man with neat regular features and thick white hair; he was wearing knitted woollen slippers, and a surprising brown and yellow plaid shirt with a black western bootlace tie. In 1945, according to John Hersey's description, he was 'a small man, quick to talk, laugh and cry ... He moves nervously and fast, but with a restraint which suggests that he is a cautious, thoughtful man.'

He handed me a twenty-two-page outline, written by himself, of his life and career. It revealed that he was born in 1909 into a Buddhist family, was converted by a Methodist missionary, much to his family's disapproval, and won a scholarship to study theology at Emory University, Atlanta, Georgia in 1937. He graduated in 1940; then came three months at a Hollywood Independent Japanese church before he was sent to Okinawa Central Methodist Church, where an American missionary introduced him to a Japanese Christian woman who became his wife. After Pearl Harbor, he was transferred to Hiroshima, where he was the minister of the Nagarekawa United Church of Christ near the station in the city centre. Incredibly, he survived the bombing unhurt, as did his wife and baby son, but most of his congregation were killed and his church was destroyed. 'The minister and his family set up a little refuge and used it for a temporary chapel and began Sunday morning services for a small group of survivors,' says his autobiographical summary. 'While we were praying I was given a vision saying, (1) our church should be rebuilt on this ruins, (2) our sermons should be backed up with practical means of Christian love for the survivors, (3) the Peace movement should be carried out through our personal experiences of the Hiroshima disaster.'

John Hersey movingly describes how the Reverend Tanimoto, with great courage, tried to help the badly wounded victims of the bombing; at the end of his account he reports that the Reverend was thinking about how to raise money to rebuild his church. Former classmates of his from Atlanta, Georgia, read the Hersey story and felt, as did many other American readers, that they must do something to help. 'I began to receive good letters, from America,' the Reverend Tanimoto told me. 'Some of my friends from Emory read about me, and they said, "Wow! Tanimoto in Hiroshima! Let's get him over here!" ' As a result, the Reverend Tanimoto went to America in 1948 and spent eighteen months on a lecture tour raising money for his church. He met and impressed a number of journalists during the trip; one of them was Norman Cousins, editor of the *Saturday Review*.

Cousins was a prolific writer and campaigner who had already questioned America's decision to use nuclear weapons against Japan. He now gave the Reverend Tanimoto space in the *Saturday Review* and, after realising how responsive the readers were, announced the formation, in the spring of 1949, of a committee to offer support and help to Hiroshima. Thus was born the

Hiroshima Peace Center Associates. Among the members were John Hersey, the novelist Pearl Buck, and the Reverend Tanimoto himself. Later that year, Cousins paid his first visit to Hiroshima, where, encouraged by the Reverend, he decided to promote an appeal in America for the five or six thousand children orphaned by the bomb. Back in New York he launched the Moral Adoption Scheme, whereby American benefactors sponsored and corresponded with an orphan, sending gifts and money regularly. The scheme received wide publicity and made a powerful impression on public opinion in Japan.

Meanwhile the Reverend Tanimoto had begun to take a keen interest in the scarred young women known as the Hiroshima Maidens. One or two started coming to his church, but drifted away. 'I poured my spiritual energy into encouraging these girls,' he told me, 'but they disappeared. They hated to be seen.' He decided that they needed a special group of their own where they would not be subjected to curious stares; in 1951 he started a Bible study group exclusively for them. 'I told them, study the Bible!' he said, fiercely. 'You have to stand on your own two feet! In order to do so you have to know God's love!'

Among the young women who came to the Reverend Tanimoto's Bible classes were Shigeko, Toyoko and Michiko Y. Not all the participants were Christian, and the ones I met told me that they regarded the class more as a general support group than a religious assembly. They found the meetings comforting. 'It was good to realise that there were others with the same problems,' said one girl. 'We could talk together about the things that bothered us, about whether we should give up all ideas of getting married, or about how it felt when we saw our younger sisters starting to have boyfriends. We understood each other's feelings.' The Reverend Tani-

moto also did his best to find work for the girls. Three of
them started to help run another of his projects, a home
for blind children.

Around this time, in Tokyo, a well-known novelist,
Shizuye Masugi, had become a member of a women's
group interested in doing something for the Hiroshima
Maidens. She asked the Reverend Tanimoto how she
and her associates could help, and he suggested trying to
raise funds for plastic surgery. The PEN Club took up
the campaign, and enough money was raised to send
nine girls to Tokyo in 1952 for treatment; the following
year, twelve more were treated in Osaka. But then,
according to the Reverend Tanimoto, the money seemed
to dry up. 'Orphans always popular; Maidens not so,'
said Tanimoto briskly. 'Needed much money. My
friends encouraged me to go to foundations to ask for
money for girls; they didn't give.'

Feeling that he had exhausted the possibilities of
finding help for the scarred women in Japan, the
Reverend Tanimoto began to think of appealing to some
of his friends in America.

Part 2

America, 1953–6

6

The Hiroshima Maidens Project

After nearly forty years, I discovered, people in Japan and the United States are still wondering why Norman Cousins took up the cause of the Hiroshima atomic bomb casualties. Certainly among his motives, as for many of the Americans who were to help him with the Hiroshima Maidens project, was guilt. 'I found it difficult to digest the fact that the United States was the first country in history to drop the atomic bomb on human beings,' he has written. 'Seeing Hiroshima was an experience that changed my life.' His intervention in Hiroshima was to affect many lives besides his own.

By the early 1950s, Cousins had been editing the *Saturday Review* for ten years. He was born in New Jersey in 1915 into a middle-class family; as a small boy he was sent to a sanatorium with suspected tuberculosis, and he has said that his drive to make the world a better place originated in the realisation that while he was getting better, some of the other children would not survive. He went to Teachers College at Columbia University in New York and found a job in 1936 as Education Correspondent for the *New York Post*. He joined the *Saturday Review* in 1940. During the war he edited an international magazine sponsored by the US government.

By 1953 Cousins was living with his wife Ellen and their four daughters in a big old wooden house in New Canaan, Connecticut. Cousins had transformed the *Saturday Review* from a literary magazine into a journal of ideas and world affairs. Ambitious and energetic, he wrote prolifically and travelled a great deal; his staff found it hard to keep up with him. He felt he had a special relationship with Hiroshima, where since the Moral Adoption scheme he had launched in 1949 he had become known as Moral Parent number I.

When the Reverend Tanimoto took the Cousins to meet some of the Hiroshima Maidens in the basement room at his church one evening in August 1953, the group had been meeting there for two years. They knew that it was the Reverend Tanimoto, with his indefatigable determination to organise publicity, funding and treatment for bomb victims, who had arranged for several of them to be taken to Tokyo or Osaka for surgery; they must also have been aware of the success of his campaign for the orphans, who were largely supported by money from American benefactors.

In some quarters in Japan, the Reverend Tanimoto was by now under attack for his activities. Why was so much fuss being made about the victims of Hiroshima, when so many other Japanese had suffered badly during the war? Wasn't there something rather humiliating about his lecture tours, in which he asked Japan's former enemies for charity? And didn't he himself seem to be rather too keen on the drama and publicity? At one stage, the Reverend Tanimoto has recalled, his wife was so unnerved by the hostility building up towards her husband that she asked him to abandon the campaign for the Maidens. But he felt there was a good chance that his friend Norman Cousins would be able to do something more for the scarred women, and he was already hoping that perhaps treatment might be arranged for them in the United States.

Norman and Ellen Cousins met, they recall, eight or nine young women that evening. Among them was Shigeko; both the Americans were particularly taken with her. Even though she was one of the most disfigured, with the bottom half of her face nearly obliterated by a large dark-red scar, she was, Cousins remembers, 'very winning and open'. She sat next to Ellen Cousins as the group talked, through an interpreter, about their lives, their problems and also about their feelings towards America.

Looking back, the Cousins were less shocked by the women's scars than moved by the limited lives the group were obliged to lead. They were also touched by the women's apparent lack of resentment towards America and Americans. Perhaps their attitudes were conditioned by their passion for American movies, which occupied a lot of their time. It was dark in the cinema, so no one could stare at their faces; and they could indulge in romantic, if for us painfully ironic, fantasies. 'We like to see the pretty American girls and imagine that we are they,' Cousins remembers one girl saying. Ellen Cousins told me that what stayed in her mind was how mad they all seemed to be about Gary Cooper, and how one of them said to her: 'When he kisses a girl, I just imagine he's kissing me.'

Ellen Cousins was also struck by how quickly the young women seemed to respond to their interest and how eagerly they answered direct, even personal enquiries. 'It surprised me to have them open up and talk to Norman when he started joking with them about boyfriends and so on,' she said.

Another thing touched her very much. Before she and her husband left, they asked the group if they could send them anything from America. Most of them asked for movie and fashion magazines, but Shigeko, who had been looking with particular attention at the family snaps that Ellen Cousins had passed round, said she would like to keep the pictures.

Shigeko remembers the incident slightly differently. 'I

happened to be sitting next to her, and when she asked us what we wanted from America, I didn't want anyting. Nothing! I was just looking at the pictures; and you know I used to be a great dreamer, making story in the head all the time, like who did I belong to? Which family? Or I dreamed I am very small and a big giant step on me. I was looking at the pictures, making story in my head, about if I was part of *this* family, how would I feel? Mrs Cousins thought I wanted to keep the picture, so she gave it to me.'

Cousins remembers that the idea of possible treatment for these women in America was brought up by the Reverend Tanimoto during that meeting. 'He said the girls had read about advances in plastic surgery in the United States and hoped for the miracle that would enable them to come to America . . . There was something akin to a sense of transport in their voices. I knew I would have to be careful about creating false expectations.' He said he would see what could be done. Both the Cousins left the meeting feeling that, somehow, something must be organised to help these young women. Mrs Cousins especially, touched by Shigeko and thinking of her own four daughters, wanted to make the dream come true.

When I went to talk to Norman Cousins about his part in setting up the project – for it was he and the Reverend Tanimoto between them who did the groundwork – I had recently been looking at his 1945 polemic against atomic war, *Modern Man is Obsolete*. One statement in it had struck me as possibly the clue to why he took up the Reverend Tanimoto's suggestion: 'The quintessence of destruction as potentially represented by modern science must be dramatised and kept in the forefront of public opinion.' Was his motive, in helping some of the victims of Hiroshima, to do just that?

Cousins today looks very little different from how he

appears in the photographs taken on his visits to Hiroshima in the late 1940s and early 1950s. He is a smallish man, not particularly impressive until he focuses his intent brown eyes on you and starts to put his point across. He speaks slowly, thoughtfully, and with some weight.

'Philosophically, the bombing did not rest easily with me,' he said. 'This —' he paused, looking for the right word — 'anguish increased the more I learned about the circumstances of the dropping of the bomb.' He outlined for me the main reasons why he, and others, have questioned the American action: there should surely, he said, have been a demonstration of the power of the bomb, especially after the Chicago scientists who had worked on it wrote to President Truman recommending that this should be done. There was also evidence that after Yalta the United States was determined to clinch victory over the Japanese in the Pacific before Russia came in against Japan and staked a claim there. He decided, he said, that 'the rationale that the motive for dropping the bomb was to save American lives was a colossal deceit . . . Therefore, the people of Hiroshima and Nagasaki, it seemed to me, the people who were killed, were more victimised by a chronology of international politique than by the given reason. I found this very difficult to swallow, as an American.' So had he been conscious of a deeper motive than simply the humanitarian impulse to arrange treatment for some innocent victims of the American strategy? He nodded. 'At the time I presented it as a mission of mercy; but there was a fire in my belly. There was no other symbolism that could be put to work at the time.' So the Maidens were symbols, to him, of the need to stir America's conscience? 'They were also very plucky, lovely young ladies,' he said quickly. 'Here were people who needed help; we were in a position to provide it. It seemed to me that we needed a connection between the two.'

Cousins was also struck by the way the women seemed to assume that he, as an American, could do anything he set his mind to. 'At the end of the war, Americans were regarded as some kind of a super-race, I guess,' he said. 'Of course the Japanese had seen the United States as the model, even when they went to war against us.' He wanted to use this position of power that America had acquired in the minds of ordinary Japanese in a constructive way; he also wanted very much to do something to counteract, and possibly even ultimately to change, the invidious role of the Atomic Bomb Casualty Commission in Hiroshima. 'One of the things that most troubled me about the American medical presence in Hiroshima and Nagasaki was that we were reporting on the effects of the atomic bomb but not treating them,' he said. 'I admired a great many of the American doctors there, who found a way very often to treat survivors even though they were not supposed to; but in general the result of our policy there was that the treatment of survivors was handled as a problem of politics and diplomacy and not, as it should have been, as a problem of human compassion.' Cousins was referring here to the American government's policy, which determined the ABCC's position, that to treat the victims of Hiroshima and Nagasaki would be to acknowledge the special horror of atomic bomb injuries. It was feared that this would give credibility to the anti-nuclear lobby, which Washington was trying to contain.

Both Norman Cousins and the Reverend Tanimoto, from their different perspectives, were strongly anti-Communist. Both were aware that the end of the Occupation and the release of previously inaccessible information about the effects of the atomic bombings had supplied pro-Communist and anti-American political groups in Japan with plenty of useful material. Cousins' and the Reverend Tanimoto's wish to help the Hiroshima Maidens for humanitarian reasons was bolstered by a strong desire to show America in a more favourable light. The lifting of restrictions on information coming out of Hiroshima coincided with a wave of extreme alarm there about the incidence of radiation-induced leukaemia, which had been increasing in the late 1940s and reached a peak between 1950 and 1953; it was apparent that earlier ABCC reports saying that there would be no further bad news about delayed consequences of the bombings were over-optimistic. Among their motives in launching the project was certainly the desire to do something positive and helpful not only for the survivors but for the image of the United States in Japan. Cousins later told an American journalist that the Reverend Tanimoto was worried by anti-American rumours circulating in Japan about the United States' motives in dropping the bombs: 'I do not speculate on such things because I have no knowledge,' the Reverend Tanimoto was quoted as saying. 'But what I do know is that the American people have been just and generous to Japan in defeat. And I have great confidence in America because I have studied there and been there since the end of the war. I am certain that if by some miracle these girls could be given the medical treatment they so badly need it would be a wonderful thing for both countries.' Cousins told the reporter that he saw the project as 'a powerful symbol of goodwill. Such a symbol was urgently needed in view of ugly movements against the United States then starting up in Japan.'

Among his archives at his house in California Norman Cousins has several large scrapbooks and a number of bulging folders concerning the background to and progress of the Hiroshima Maidens project. From this mass of detail one fact emerges clearly: every kind of obstacle was placed in the way of the scheme, but Cousins, once committed to bringing the women to America, was determined to make it happen. From the correspondence it appeared that when his associates and supporters raised problems, he rose above them, solved them or ignored them. He has had, I discovered, something of a reputation for initiating projects and then moving on so fast that other people were left wondering how to fulfil the promises he had made; but however much strain his behaviour may have placed on his colleagues and staff, he usually managed to get his way.

After discussing the idea with the other Peace Center Associates and getting their support, Cousins began to investigate the possibility of financial backing from foundations and institutions. 'Any number of foundations expressed sympathy,' Cousins reported later, 'but said their charters did not provide for mercy projects of this particular nature.' One was concerned that if a Maiden should die on the operating table the foundation would be held responsible. He was asked about the political views of the women: what if one of them were a Communist? And would it not be invidious to choose a small group of survivors for special treatment? What about all the others? The project might cause resentment and jealousy. They were, of course, planning to help only a very small number of the casualties, and not even in Hiroshima itself. Some of these fears were reasonable in the circumstances. Cousins was not deterred, however, by any such anxieties; nor was he impressed by the State Department's refusal to give the plan its official approval.

The State Department's main objection to the project was, Cousins heard later, that the arrival in America of a group of scarred young women from Hiroshima would create a wave of publicity about the awful and lasting effects of the weapon that the United States had used to end the war against Japan, and possibly lead to a call for massive aid. This, the government believed, would make wonderful propaganda for anti-nuclear groups and peace campaigners, most of whom were under suspicion of being pro-Communist. It was also directly counter to the official American line about the atomic bombings, sustained consistently since 1945; that the atomic bombs were legitimate weapons of war and that no implication of special guilt should attach to their use. Since Cousins in fact wanted to remind the country how appalling nuclear weapons were, he was not much moved by these arguments.

It had been clear for several years that Cold War politics had cast a shadow on the activities of the Hiroshima Peace Center Associates. After September 1949, when the Soviet Union revealed that it too had a nuclear capability, anti-nuclear and peace movements in the United States began to be regarded with suspicion. When the Korean War broke out in January 1950 the situation became even more complicated. The Peace Center had organised a petition to President Truman, signed by 100,000 survivors of the Hiroshima bombing; Cousins, the Reverend Tanimoto and John Hersey had intended to present it to the President in person, but were told that he could not accept it. The ceremonies and demonstrations planned for the fifth anniversary of the bombing in August 1950 had been cancelled. Such actions, in Cousins' opinion, would only feed anti-Americanism in Japan.

He was also informed, he told me, that the State Department's Japanese experts had grave doubts about the capacity of a group of vulnerable, unsophisticated Japanese women to adapt to strange surroundings and go through the ordeal of surgery in a foreign country. It was pointed out to him that the food and social customs of America would be totally different and probably disagreeable to the Japanese women, leaving aside the language problem. However, Cousins remembered the eagerness with which the women he had already met had talked of American films and fashions.

It became plain to him during the first six months after his return from Hiroshima in 1953 that the project would have to be organised and funded privately without government help or endorsement. One of Cousins' greatest friends was his doctor, William Hitzig, a large, flamboyant New York general practitioner with a flair for publicity, a fine house on Fifth Avenue, a love of fast cars and good food, and a profound admiration for Cousins' humanitarian and statesmanlike qualities. The two men discussed the Hiroshima Maidens and what was needed to get the project off the ground. Hitzig said he would like to take it up with his friend Dr Arthur Barsky, one of America's leading plastic surgeons and head of the plastic surgery division at Mount Sinai Hospital in Manhattan. I was told that Dr Barsky, who died in 1982, was as quiet and low key as Dr Hitzig was effervescent; but he was a man of great kindness and great distinction, and everyone I talked to in America and Japan remembered him with special respect and affection. He decided that if the governing body of Mount Sinai agreed, he and his department would undertake the treatment of a group of young women from Hiroshima free of charge. The hospital gave its permission.

Although the arrangement with Mount Sinai and Dr Barsky was a tremendous breakthrough, Cousins still had daunting problems. How would the group travel? There was no question of them paying their own fares, or living expenses while not in hospital. Where, indeed, would they live? For a time it looked as if he might have found the solution in the co-operation of the Girl Scouts of America.

By a strange coincidence, Cousins received a letter in the autumn of 1953 from Janet Tobitt, then director of the Far East section of the Girl Scouts movement. 'You probably know there is at present a great deal of "anti-Americanism" propagated by the Communists, and a friend and I have been wondering what new act of goodwill might counteract it. They have made a great play of the mutilated features of girls from the blast who now grown up cannot get jobs or marry ...' Janet Tobitt had supported the Moral Adoption programme; she now suggested that something similar might be done for the Hiroshima Maidens.

Over the next few months she and Cousins corresponded about the possibility that the Girl Scouts might play a part in looking after the girls in America. Janet Tobitt was tremendously enthusiastic. Then, in the spring of 1954, her tone changed. She was still personally committed, but 'All sorts of difficulties have arisen ... the matter is most delicate ...' Somehow, any notion that the Girl Scouts could be officially connected with the project had become unlikely.

Cousins assumed that this unease stemmed from the State Department. It was inevitable that when government-related organisations asked advice from Washington about whether they should help him or not, they would get an off-putting response. Then in March 1954 something happened that made world headlines, embarrassed the Americans, incensed the Japanese and transformed the fragmented Japanese anti-nuclear and peace movement. A Japanese fishing boat, the *Lucky Dragon*, operating in the area round Bikini Atoll in the Pacific where the United States was holding hydrogen bomb tests, was showered for six hours with radioactive ash. By mid-March, all twenty-three crew members were ill with radiation sickness. The cargo of fish was also found to be heavily contaminated.

During most of 1954, while Norman Cousins was trying to work out the problems of transport, accommodation and funds for the Hiroshima Maidens, the consequences and repercussions of the *Lucky Dragon* incident continued. In April, the Diet in Japan passed resolutions calling for an international ban on nuclear weapons, and a group of Tokyo housewives started a campaign to gather signatures for an appeal. Called the Suginami Appeal after their district, it had amassed 18 million names by November. Meanwhile, in Hiroshima, activists among the various small survivor groups were pointing out, with some bitterness, that the radiation sickness which the fishermen were enduring to the fascinated horror of the nation, was all too familiar to them. In May, Hiroshima held a 'Citizens Conference against Atomic and Hydrogen Bombs', and passed the first resolution asking the Japanese government to pay for victims' medical costs. There seemed, at last, to be a tide of interest and support flowing towards *hibakusha*.

In America, all this made the government even more sensitive to the damaging propaganda expected if the Maidens ever came to New York. In Japan too the situation became more complex and delicate than before. What had seemed to most of the Americans, and the more Americanised of the Japanese concerned, like the Reverend Tanimoto, to be a constructive, public gesture from a small group of Americans to a small group of Japanese, began in the wake of the *Lucky Dragon* incident to look like an obvious attempt to win favour and create good publicity. A clumsy gesture by another American in Hiroshima during this time caused a storm of indignation. The director of the Atomic Bomb Casualty Commission, Dr John Morton, offered to treat the crew of the *Lucky Dragon* at the clinic.

Nothing, as another American academic working there, Herbert Passin, wrote later, could have been more tactless at the time.

> For years the American government had been using all its resources in the field of public relations to tell the Japanese that the ABCC had not been set up in order to cure people, that it had no facilities for giving treatment and that this was how it had to be . . . the Japanese had never quite got over their suspicions that they were being used as guinea-pigs by the ABCC. Therefore one of two conclusions must be drawn from the ABCC's offer: either the Commission's previous statement that it was incapable of giving medical treatment was a lie; or else the Americans wished to make use of this latest catastrophe for their own research purposes . . . Dozens of articles appeared in the press, all with the same theme: 'We won't be treated like guinea-pigs.'

Similar suspicions were attached to the Maidens idea. What would the Americans really be doing to the girls? Would they be helping them – or studying them? Why did they have to be taken to America? Why didn't the Americans organise treatment in Hiroshima? Then there was the question of the hurt pride involved for Japanese surgeons; a number of them denied that any more was known in the USA than in Japan about plastic surgery, especially about the special problems of operating on keloids.

Cousins, however, was not deflected – possibly because much of this anxiety did not reach him in New York. He was still wrestling with the practical details; nevertheless, early in 1955 he felt confident enough to write to the Mayor of Hiroshima making an official offer to treat about twenty girls, free, in New York. The Mayor's response was positive, but he had two serious reservations: the selection process would have to be

69

handled very carefully, and he feared that to take only young women would arouse envy, especially among scarred boys and young men. Meanwhile the American Embassy in Tokyo was also expressing concern. A contact from Hiroshima wrote to Cousins: 'Because of the propaganda that could result if any cases fail, the Ambassador thought it wise for the doctors to come here and make their selection from the girls whose operations would be successful. To have even one failure would be bad publicity.' It was agreed that Cousins, Dr Hitzig and Dr Barsky would all go personally to Hiroshima to choose the girls.

The project was gathering momentum. The matter of transportation was solved after Janet Tobitt, still helping unofficially, suggested to Cousins that he approach the president of the *Nippon Times*, Kiyoshi Togasaki. The paper, now the *Japan Times*, was and still is Japan's main English-language newspaper, and reflects the most influential pro-American political viewpoint. Togasaki took the view that the project could only create good propaganda, threw his weight behind it and asked his friend General Hull, who after the end of the Occupation had been given the post of commander of the US Air Force in Japan, if he would provide a plane. To everyone's surprise, the General said yes. Finally, Cousins came up with the solution to the most serious remaining problem: how and where the women were to live. He approached the Friends, the American Quakers, and asked for their help. On 11 April 1955 the Executive Committee of the Friends Center in New York agreed to take on the responsibility for finding homes for the girls in the New York area.

The addition of the Quakers to the project's support system was inspired. They were conscientious, reliable people who had one outstanding asset as hosts and friends to a party of scarred Japanese war victims; as

Quakers they were pacifists, who had neither fought in nor supported the Second World War. There was also a strong tradition in the Quaker movement of unobtrusive testimonial to belief in God and God's love through individual actions of kindness and hospitality. The New York Meeting contacted the local Meetings of Quakers in outer suburban areas in New York, Connecticut and New Jersey, explaining the project and asking for help. Some Quakers were daunted; they might be idealists, but they could see all sorts of risks and dangers. But on the whole the response was encouraging. The New York Meeting found a volunteer, Ida Day, to act as co-ordinator of possible host families. Ida Day was then in her mid-forties and had been involved for many years with Quaker social work. She was married to a paediatrician and had two teenage daughters.

In the early spring of 1955, after nearly two years of uncertainty, the Hiroshima Maidens project started to become a reality. Despite some critical rumblings from his community, the Mayor of Hiroshima decided to accept Norman Cousins' invitation; he set up a local committee to discuss plans for the selection and departure of about twenty young women. It was decided that it was important to offer the chance of treatment in America to a wider group than the Reverend Tanimoto's Bible class; there were already hostile whispers that the Reverend had too much influence with Cousins, that it was unfair if only Christian girls were to go, and that it was all another stunt by the Reverend to raise more money for his church and his pet projects. Accordingly, doctors like Dr Harada who knew of scarred survivors were asked to recommend candidates, and towards the end of March, shortly before the arrival of the Cousins party, announcements were made on radio and in the local press inviting young women to attend the Hiroshima Citizens' Hospital for interviews and examinations.

In Washington, the unwelcome Hiroshima Maidens project was beginning to look like a *fait accompli*. The State Department kept trying to contain it; a newsletter sent out by the Hiroshima Peace Center Associates on 19 March announced that the wheels were in motion and carried a nervous postscript from an official:

> May I speak a word of caution on this point. The State Department has insisted that we keep the coming of the A-Bomb victims to New York as secret as possible. They feel that tabloid exploitation will greatly damage our relations with the Japanese as a nation and only bring comfort to the communists. Your co-operation in this respect will be appreciated.

However, Walter S. Robertson, Assistant Secretary of State for the Far East, wrote a few days later to the Director of Mount Sinai Hospital: 'I believe this project can have a helpful effect on our relations with Japan . . .'

7

The Group Is Chosen

On 10 April Cousins and his party arrived in Tokyo. He
had with him, as well as Dr Barsky and Dr Hitzig, a
woman nurse from Mount Sinai Hospital and Candis
Hitzig, the doctor's eighteen-year-old daughter who, it
was announced, was acting as secretary to the enterprise. Cousins later admitted that he was taken aback by
the great interest shown by the Japanese press not
merely in what he was doing, but why. He was repeatedly interviewed by journalists; some of the questions, he
said, were 'severe'. Was he being secretly financed by the
US government in an attempt to offset the bad publicity
caused by the *Lucky Dragon* incident? Was he going to
raise money by exhibiting the girls as freaks around
America? Were American doctors going to use the girls
for research? Why was he taking only girls? Was
Japanese medical expertise inferior to American?
Cousins dealt with all these questions calmly. He explained that the project was entirely a private initiative:
'I wish to stress that neither the American nor Japanese
government has any responsibility for the project itself.'
There was no question of exhibiting the girls or using
them as guinea-pigs. He and his wife had been especially
touched by the girls and young women of Hiroshima
because they had four daughters themselves. 'In attempt-
ing to do something on behalf of the girls we did not
intend to discriminate against others equally needy.' He
was particularly delicate in his reference to Japanese
medical skills. 'Since the American doctors will provide

73

surgical treatment of an order not yet given the girls, there is no question here of either the Japanese doctors or surgeons losing face. All the members of this volunteer project have the greatest admiration for Japanese medicine.'

He was also asked: what were the criteria for choosing the girls? 'Many factors are involved,' he said. 'Do the girls have the kind of burns or contractions that have a reasonably good chance of being improved? What about the general health of the girls in view of the extensive undertaking involved? Do they appear to have the kind of emotional stability required to enable them to adjust easily to new surroundings and experiences? The final determination will be made not by the Americans alone, but by joint decision of Americans and Japanese.'

Behind this careful, tactful reply lay one of the most sensitive issues of all. The girls had to be visibly scarred enough to be in evident need of surgery, but not so badly scarred as to pose too difficult a task for the plastic surgeons. Above all, 'general health' in this context meant that they must not be suffering from any variety of radiation sickness. Three people had died already that year in Hiroshima of illnesses related to the atomic bomb, and a fourth was dying that very week of a blood disorder; all such cases received wide publicity in Japan.

Forty-three women applied to be interviewed. After examining and talking to them, the American and Japanese doctors chose twenty, with a reserve list of five, all of whom were eventually included. Eighteen were turned down. Forty years later, I asked the women I met how they had felt about the prospect of going to America for treatment; I was struck by how many of them remembered having had reservations.

Terue, whose father had made her massage her scars, had never been to the Reverend Tanimoto's church; it was her father who had seen the announcement in the newspaper and taken her to see Dr Harada. 'I had mixed feelings,' she said. 'I did feel some fear, but also I so badly wanted something done for my face. I wanted to get my face back.' Michiko, who had clung to her mother on the deserted beach, remembers that she would not have had the courage to think of going to America if her mother had not pushed her: 'My mother wanted us to do anything that would improve my face.'

Shigeko wondered whether she could tolerate more operations; she had had several in Tokyo on her hands, which had improved, and on her face, which seemed much the same. She hated the thought of more skin being taken from other parts of her scarred body. 'We had interviews,' she told me. 'They said to me, "You want to go to America?" I said, "I don't know." They were surprised! They said, "Why not?" I said I had already too many operations. But when they say, "If you were chosen, would you go?" I said yes.' Norman Cousins told me that the doctors were very doubtful about taking Shigeko; there was indeed very little unburned skin or 'suitable donor tissue' on her body. But he had grown attached to her, and he persuaded them that she should be included.

Toyoko, one of the oldest, was by this time in her late twenties and studying dress design at a school in Tokyo. She too had had several operations and found the results disappointing; she was not at all sure about going to America.

'While I was in Tokyo I got a card from the City government, to say that Dr Barsky and Norman Cousins were coming and asking me to go for an interview. At first, I didn't want to go; and even when I was chosen, I was doubtful. One of my friends, a boy who lived in Tokyo, he said, "Don't go! It's like a . . . [she got up to search for the word she wanted in a dictionary] like a

75

sideshow, in a circus." But then the Reverend Tanimoto
told me I should go, because America had good plastic
surgery, better than Japan.' She talked it over with two
of the other women and they decided to accept. 'But I
was always thinking, I'll be back in Tokyo in maybe half
a year. I didn't expect to stay long; I was attending
school. I liked living in Tokyo, I was happier, there were
not so many people watching us.'

Some of the women's families were not overjoyed at
the prospect of their vulnerable daughters being taken
so far away, to be treated by their former enemies for
injuries inflicted by those enemies. Toyoko's mother
was among them. 'She didn't want me to go. She hated
America. I don't like to say it, but in those days – it's
different now, of course – well, she had lost a son in the
war, and then my father died, and then there was me,
and we lost our homes and everything, and my mother
was very upset and she would always say oh, I *hate*
America.' When I said to Toyoko that it seemed to me
understandable, indeed natural, that her mother should
have felt like that, she looked at me sadly and said, 'I
know. It was war. Japan was bad too.'

For Michiyo, who had been injured on her way to
work, the decision was apparently much simpler. She
had found a job, eventually, after reading an article in a
magazine advising young women in the post-war world
to branch out and try to be self-sufficient; it was a
clerical job in a vocational training centre. She had never
been to the Reverend Tanimoto's church; the first she
heard of the project was when she saw a newspaper
story in her office. 'I just ran out of there right away,'
she told me. 'It was the last day of the interviews, and I
ran all the way to the hospital. I was so very much
hoping they could do something for my arm.' She was
put on the reserve list.

Cousins and the other Americans felt concerned

about the eighteen who had been turned down. The evening before the final selection was made, most of the candidates attended a special church service where the Reverend Tanimoto led them in prayers for the American doctors, that they might not feel pain at not being able to take all the women. They also prayed for those of them who would not be chosen. When I asked Cousins whether it had not been very difficult, even painful, to have to choose some girls and reject others, he said: 'Yes, it was. We didn't want to jeopardise the entire project by taking more than we knew we could treat successfully.'

In Hiroshima, when I asked if it would be possible for me to talk to any of the rejected candidates, it turned out that one of them, Miyoko, now works as a librarian in the Peace Memorial Library. She is a small, bustling woman with short black hair and an eager expression; her face does not now look badly scarred, although there are traces of burns around her eyes and mouth. She seemed different from the other women I had met; her feelings were much nearer the surface. She had shared the same terrible experience as the others; she had been badly burned as a schoolgirl of twelve. Later, as a teenager, she had joined the Reverend Tanimoto's group and been sent to Tokyo and then to Osaka for surgery to her eyelids and to a badly deformed hand. When the Cousins project was announced, she was working with two other scarred girls in the home for blind children started by the Reverend Tanimoto. 'He was afraid that we would not find a job because of the keloids on our faces,' she told me, 'so he started this home and these jobs.' All three applied to go to America: the other two were accepted, and she was not. Her eyes filled with tears. 'I was the only one left out: I was so unhappy,' she said, her voice trembling. Why did she think they had rejected her? 'I was kicked out because of my emotional problems,' she said. 'I was very worried about my family. My elder brother was very sick, so I felt very sorry to think of leaving for America.' But at the same time, she had wanted to go? 'Of course I wanted to go. My feelings were all mixed up. If my family circumstances had been different, I could have gone.'

It was not hard to sympathise with the doctors, I thought, who must have feared that the strain of worrying about her family would be too much for Miyoko; but it also appeared that being turned down had not assisted her emotional balance. It was also clear that she, and presumably the other rejected candidates, thought that their turn would come next. Norman Cousins left Hiroshima saying that he would do what he could for them, that treatment would somehow be arranged. The Americans felt they had made no specific promises. But when I asked Miyoko if she and the others felt that they too would have a chance to go to America for treatment, she said without hesitation, 'Of course.'

After the choices had been made, Norman Cousins and Dr Hitzig flew on to Indonesia to attend a conference. They would be back in New York well before the group's arrival, in two or three weeks' time. Dr Barsky and the others stayed in Hiroshima to help organise the departure, although they also intended to do some sightseeing while in Japan. There were some important decisions still to make about who should accompany the girls, look after them and interpret for them. It was at this point that a Japanese-American woman, Helen Yokoyama, became involved with the group. She was to do perhaps more than anyone else to influence the course of the next eighteen months, and her impact on everyone concerned can be felt to this day.

Helen Yokoyama was then in her mid-forties, working as an interpreter in the Atomic Bomb Casualty

Commission. Today, in her seventies, she lives most of the year in the fine old wooden house that belonged to her husband's family, in the mountains to the north of Hiroshima. She is a small woman with great dignity and presence, whose background, education and experiences have made her a remarkable combination of the independent American and the traditional Japanese. This background made her almost uncannily suitable for the role of interpreter not just of language but of two different outlooks and cultures.

She was born in Berkeley, California, and is an American citizen. Her parents were from the Hiroshima area, and had settled in the USA where her father ran his own business. When she was twelve they did what good Japanese families living abroad liked to do if they could afford it; they sent her back to learn, as she puts it, 'how to be a proper Japanese young lady. Only I never did quite learn.' She found it very hard, she says, but she settled down. She had hoped to go on to a leading girls' college in Hiroshima, but on a visit to her parents in California during the Depression she realised that the business was not going as well as it had. So she stayed and went to the University of California at Berkeley instead, where she studied psychology and English literature. Soon after she graduated, she married; her husband was Japanese, from an old landed family. Together they went back to Tokyo; she had three children, a son and two daughters.

When the war came, her position was painful. Her parents were sent to a relocation camp in California; she and her husband left Tokyo and went to live in the country with his family. He was against the war, she told me. For years he had belonged to a Christian pacifist group that held meetings in secret. He managed to avoid military service by taking a vital job with the national electricity company; she found herself, with three young children, looking after his elderly parents and running a fair-sized farm with no help. She heard the atomic bomb explode on 6 August 1945, and her area was soon receiving wounded refugees and being asked to send help to the stricken city. With her perfect English and her American connections, it was natural that she should find herself offered work at the Atomic Bomb Casualty Commission, where she rediscovered the American manners she had abandoned for ten years.

'I'd gone back to the old Japanese fashion,' she told me. 'Never look a person in the eye, it's very rude; and never show your teeth when you laugh.' She demonstrated a traditional polite Japanese titter behind her hand, eyes demurely lowered. 'A colleague at the ABCC, an American woman, called me in one day and said: "Helen, you're the only Japanese employee with a good American education. Take pride in yourself! Look me straight in the eye!" I owe a great deal to her.'

Helen Yokoyama, despite working at the Atomic Bomb Casualty Commission, had never, she said later, taken a particular interest in bomb victims. 'So many people had died in that war, and I even used to question why those *hibakusha* had to receive special treatment.' Then, one day in April 1955, she was asked to help sort out the inoculation problems of two visiting Americans. Norman Cousins and Dr Hitzig had not had time to have the second round of injections then required before they left America. 'They were a bit surprised that a middle-aged Japanese woman spoke English so well,' said Helen. Soon she was asked if she would consider accompanying the Hiroshima Maidens to the United States, to interpret and to look after them. She was hesitant; it would mean at least six months away from her family, and her younger daughter was only twelve. She was inclined to refuse; but Dr Hitzig's daughter, Candis, begged her at least to go along one evening to meet the women and help Candis talk to them. She was trying to give them regular conversation lessons in rudimentary English and to tell them a little about American family life.

'I went along with her to Tanimoto's church,' said Helen. 'In a gloomy, dark room, sitting round a long table, I saw twenty-four girls, all waiting. As we went in, they all looked at us, naturally. It was such a shock to me, I can't tell you.' It was not their scars that struck her, but their expressions. 'There was no light in their eyes; they looked so afraid. They looked to me like puppies left outside in the rain with their tails hanging down.' She sat down and talked a little to the group, and began to feel that she might have to go with them after all. 'I was thinking — I can't let these girls go off like this, at such short notice, knowing nothing of the country or the language.' After a while she noticed another young woman, Hiroko T., who had arrived late and seemed to be hanging back, nervously. She wore a large mask covering the whole lower part of her face. When tea was brought, Helen saw that Hiroko's mouth was so deformed that she could not open it to drink. At that moment, Helen made up her mind to go. When she asked her husband what he thought, he said: 'We should not be selfish. None of our children was hurt in the war.' And her younger daughter said to her: 'I have a father and a grandmother here. Please help these poor girls.'

Someone else who was trying to make up his mind about joining the Hiroshima Maidens on their journey was Dr Tomin Harada. He had helped Dr Barsky and Dr Hitzig to examine the women and had given them his advice about the special problems of treating keloid scars; they had invited him to go to New York to help with the operations. He was doubtful; it would mean leaving his hospital and his other patients for several months at least. It would also mean accepting a secondary role in the treatment of the group, several of whom he had already operated on himself. He shared some of the Hiroshima community's anxieties about the project; above all, the fear that the women's hopes might be unrealistic and that they might be subjected to undesirable publicity. 'I was much concerned,' he told me. 'My thoughts were mixed. I decided to consult Professor Osada from Hiroshima University.'

Osada was himself a *hibakusha*, and an academic of great distinction who had compiled a powerful collection of eye-witness accounts by children of the bombing. 'He said I should accept the suggestion, because it was a proposal made at the citizen level, nothing to do with the government. It was a gesture of goodwill and should be received with goodwill. Also, he said, if I accompanied the girls it would be easier for them. They would have a Japanese-speaking doctor there who they knew they could rely on. After all, I had treated hundreds of similar cases. So I decided to go, for two reasons: to respond to the goodwill of the citizens, and to observe new techniques in plastic surgery.'

8

From Hiroshima to New York

On the morning of 5 May 1955, nine years and nine months after an American plane dropped the bomb that devastated their city, killed around 100,000 of their fellow citizens and scarred their own bodies and faces, the twenty-five young women known as the Hiroshima Maidens boarded another US Air Force plane to fly to America for treatment. On the way to the airport at Iwakuni they stopped to offer prayers at the memorial in the city centre to those killed in the bombing; they were seen off by city officials as well as by their families and some of the women who were to be left behind. They were accompanied on the flight by a young reporter from the *Japan Times*, Dr Tomin Harada and a colleague, Dr Ouchi, the Reverend Tanimoto and their interpreter-cum-chaperone, Helen Yokoyama, as well as the returning American party. They were all wearing similar Western-style dark-blue travelling suits and white gloves, and had tried to curl their hair in the American manner. Each had packed one small suitcase, having been told that new clothes would be provided for them. The farewells had been restrained; it is not done in Japan to embrace or to have emotional scenes in public. The young reporter wrote in his first story for the *Japan Times* that the girls were 'happy and laughing' throughout the trip; but the ones I met remembered feeling frightened, especially when the plane started to vibrate before it took off, and soon they were all feeling rather sick.

At the last minute, despite nearly two years of preparation, the venture was almost cancelled. According to Norman Cousins, the State Department in Washington had finally decided to call the whole project off; a telegram was sent to General Hull in Tokyo, the Commander of the American Air Force in Japan, who had authorised the flight on his own initiative. 'The General said to his aide: "Unfortunately I don't have my glasses with me," ' said Cousins. 'After the plane had taken off, the General wired to the State Department saying "Your wire was received but the plane had already taken off; it would be a great embarrassment to the country to have to order it back." '

The Maidens may not have known that in official quarters in America they were not especially welcome visitors; but they cannot have failed to be aware that they were leaving some envious, suspicious people behind them as well as their anxious families. On the eve of their departure, *Chugoku Shimbun*, the main Hiroshima daily paper, commented merely that it was unfortunate that the Americans could not somehow treat all the bomb victims, and exhorted the party to be dignified and firm, and not to tolerate any attempts to make them objects of public curiosity.

Helen Yokoyama, although she was returning to the country where she had been born and partly educated, was also feeling worried and uncertain. It had begun to occur to her that she was supposed to be in charge of the girls, but that no one had explained to her what was involved; and it also seemed to her, as she saw the girls going pale, that none of the men who had organised the venture really had any grasp of the problems and pitfalls ahead. 'It was an old army plane, not very comfortable, and of course none of the girls had flown before; most of them had never been outside Hiroshima, and none had ever left Japan,' she said. 'Then they began to be sick, and they were so miserable and embarrassed; none of the men, not even the doctors, seemed to notice, so I went round with paper bags and towels and rubbed their backs and talked to them. I didn't really know the girls' names, I hadn't even *met* the doctors; I was thinking: my goodness, how naïve I am! What's this all about? What am I getting into?'

Helen Yokoyama struck me as a woman of standards, who believes in doing her duty, behaving properly especially under stress, and sticking to what she thinks is right. She knew that the Americans who met the Maidens would judge Japan by how they conducted themselves; she was also more aware than any of the young women could have been, in their excited and nervous state, with their hearts set on having their faces and bodies repaired, that Japan would eventually be judging America by their looks and behaviour. She was concerned that some of the girls were barely educated and came from humble families; she is not a snob, but background means a lot to her. 'I realised they knew no American manners, but some of them knew no Japanese manners either,' she told me crisply. 'The first thing, I decided, was to teach them all good Japanese manners. That was what I made up my mind to do.'

The journey to New York took them five days. They flew for twelve hours to Wake Island for refuelling; then via Johnston Island to Hawaii, eighteen hours later. Gradually the girls stopped feeling sick and began to relax. They started to play cards and sing. They spent two nights in Hawaii, where they had the first taste of an entirely new experience: being treated like celebrities. They were billeted in the officers' quarters and entertained in the officers' club; they were taken on a sightseeing tour by the Hawaiian Japanese community and decked with flowery leis; they went to glamorous Waikiki beach and bought postcards and souvenirs with pocket money supplied by Dr Hitzig; one night the local Japanese Women's Association made them a special sushi dinner. Then they flew on to San Francisco, where they stopped briefly and had their first sight of an American city. According to Helen Yokoyama one of the women said, as they touched down, 'But I don't see any cowboys!' Helen didn't think this was a joke.

All the women were amazed at how big, how rich and above all how undamaged America looked. 'I was very surprised,' said Toyoko, who had lived in post-war Tokyo as well as Hiroshima. 'In San Francisco, no bombs in the city! It looked as if nothing happened! In Japan, everything destroyed. In America, no! You couldn't see any sign of war. It was a very big surprise.' Masako felt much the same: 'All the Americans ate so much, no wonder they were so big and energetic. And the country was so big too. No wonder Japan lost. I thought how stupid it had been to go to war with America.'

Early the following morning, just before 9 a.m. on Monday, 9 May, the Maidens' plane landed at Mitchell Air Force Base on Long Island, just outside New York City. The women, exhausted by the long journey and the night flight, came down the ramp trying to smile but looking, to two of the people waiting for them, painfully white and tense. One was Ida Day, the Quaker volunteer who had been arranging families for the visitors to stay with; the other was Dr Bernard Simon, the youngest of the surgical team from Mount Sinai Hospital. 'When I saw them get off that plane,' said Dr Simon, now semi-retired and in his seventies, 'they were a sorry sight. It was not so much their scars, I was prepared for those; but they were bone weary and their hair was all frizzed up and they looked terrified.' Ida Day was waiting at the bottom of the steps; Helen Yokoyama remembers the relief with which the whole party saw her kind, concerned face. She gave each Maiden a hug and a word of welcome; there were tears in her eyes as she told me what she had felt. 'It was rainy and a rather dark morning,' she said. 'They all looked scared stiff and sick to their stomachs. I kept thinking that, to them, we were the enemy who had done this awful thing to them and their country.'

Before the women could rest, they had to cope with the first of many encounters with the American press. Neither the reporters nor the photographers were particularly sensitive to their exhausted and vulnerable state; they wanted dramatic photographs and telling quotes. The women remembered their anger at the photographers, who kept trying to get close-ups of the worst scars, and objected when the women shielded their faces with their hands.

The group was taken into Manhattan in an Air Force bus, with a police escort. They went straight to Mount Sinai Hospital on Fifth Avenue and 105th Street, where they found the hospital's director, Dr Martin Steinberg, and other medical staff waiting to greet them. They lined up in two rows and, as they were introduced, bowed low according to Japanese custom. There were more photographs, and then all but two of the women, who were deputed to talk to the press, went inside to rest before lunch. One spokeswoman was Toyoko; the other was Michiko S., the girl whose face had so shocked Dr Harada the first time he saw it.

According to press reports the next day, these two had been elected 'leaders' of the group. The Reverend Tanimoto acted as interpreter for them with the journalists and it seems that he had helped them prepare their remarks. 'The two girls emphasised they felt "friendship for and trust in" Americans and that they bore Americans no hatred for their injuries,' reported the *New York Herald Tribune* the next day, and went on, 'Miss

Sako, noting that the group had seen the battleship *Arizona*, sunk by the Japanese at Pearl Harbor, said: "The Japanese Navy took the first step in the last war. We survivors of Hiroshima got a terrible destruction upon us, but we should have repentance rather than hatred, and we began to hate war in general." '

After a lunch at the hospital, which tried to give them a partly Japanese meal (mixed green salad, fried shrimp, Japanese preserves, soy sauce, rice, green tea), the party was taken to a midtown hotel to rest before a reception at Dr Hitzig's house that evening. Helen Yokoyama felt somewhat amazed that arrangements were apparently still being made the day they arrived. 'No one seemed quite to know what to do with us,' she says. She also thought it might be too soon for the women to appear in public, but they were mostly pleased and excited at the prospect.

Dr Tomin Harada was staying at the Hitzigs' five-storey townhouse, and he has described the party that evening. He counted about 150 people, including the Japanese Consul-General, newspaper reporters and senior hospital staff. 'Financial supporters of the project from the Jewish community and other members of New York's upper class attended in formal attire, and Quakers came in their rather simple dress . . . Overwhelmed by all this, the girls huddled together in one corner and watched the faces of the people.' Dr Harada's account of the party reveals something of the complicated emotions of the Japanese as they first encountered the Americans' lavish and overwhelming hospitality.

The Queen of the reception was clearly Candis, the eldest daughter of the Hitzigs, rather than the Maidens from Hiroshima. Candis was just eighteen and had recently made her debut in New York society. It was announced at the reception that she personally had gone all the way to

Hiroshima to invite the girls to come for treatment. She received many approving looks. Her beauty and elegant white gown made her look as if she were queen of the ball, and contrasted sharply with the scarred faces and simple clothing of the Maidens. The difference seemed to symbolise the contrast between America, the global power, and Japan, the vanquished nation. While many watched Candis, others, especially the Quakers, embraced the Hiroshima Maidens, and I felt that at this reception I had seen a cross-section of American society.

If Dr Harada's most vivid memory of that first party is of the glowing Candis Hitzig, the Reverend Tanimoto's is of Shigeko, who demonstrated with great aplomb a hula dance she had picked up in Hawaii. The reporter from the *Japan Times* wrote to his newspaper that after dinner Norman Cousins joined in games with the Maidens, and that Dr Hitzig was the hit of the evening when he tried to join Dr Harada and the women in Japanese dancing.

Within twenty-four hours of the party's arrival, Helen Yokoyama found herself caught up in an argument over using the Maidens for publicity and fund-raising that was to flare up repeatedly over the next eighteen months. The Reverend Tanimoto was to be the subject of the immensely popular NBC television programme 'This Is Your Life', to be screened live from San Francisco on 11 May. The producers had assembled several of his American college friends, flown in part of his family from Japan, and, to add drama, obtained Captain Robert Lewis, assistant pilot of the plane that had dropped the bomb on Hiroshima, to confront the Reverend Tanimoto. Now it was proposed that an appeal be launched on the programme to raise money for the Hiroshima Maidens project; for although the hospital and surgeons were donating their services, and

89

the women were being offered free hospitality, the organisers realised that there were going to be many other costs ranging from pocket money and excursions to salaries and living expenses for the Japanese doctors. Why should not some of the Maidens appear briefly on television with the Reverend Tanimoto, and thus appeal directly to the generosity of the American viewers?

Given the sensitivity of the Japanese to anything that verged on exploitation of the women, and the specific undertaking given by Cousins that they would not be displayed to raise money, the suggestion was bound to cause trouble. Helen Yokoyama found that she knew, after all, what her role was: it was not just, as Dr Barsky had told her, to be a mother to the Maidens, it was to think on their behalf of the impact at home, in Japan, of anything their American hosts might propose. 'I knew they would be going back to Japan eventually,' she told me. 'Everyone else seemed to forget that. I was determined that nothing should happen that would make their future lives, in Japan, more difficult.' If she was to be their mother, she would guard what she saw as their best interests. She had the first of a series of awkward discussions with the Reverend Tanimoto and Dr Hitzig; both men, she felt, were too ready to go along with publicity. A compromise was reached: two of the women would go to the television studios, but they would be shown only in profile behind a screen. Their scars would not be visible. One of them would read a prepared statement.

This section of the 'This Is Your Life' programme of 11 May 1955 makes uneasy viewing today. The concerned but cheerful presenter brings on the large, embarrassed Captain Lewis and asks him about his experiences on 6 August 1945; as Lewis makes his now famous statement, 'Looking down from thousands of feet over Hiroshima all I could think of was "My God, what have we done?" ', the camera shows the small, tense face of the Reverend Tanimoto, regarding him with an anxious, almost horrified expression. The presenter then explains the Hiroshima Maidens project and says: 'Tonight we would like you to meet two of these girls, both of whom have lived through the terrors of an atomic bombing. To avoid causing them any embarrassment we'll not show you their faces.' Two dark outlines appear behind a screen; a young, halting Japanese voice says in English: 'We feel so happy that we could come to America. We are very grateful to you all for what you have done for us.' The studio audience, the presenter, and Captain Lewis all applaud. Later in the programme an appeal for financial help for the project is announced; Captain Lewis steps forward to make the first contribution.

Despite – or perhaps because of – its queasy combination of showbusiness and guilt, the programme had a tremendous impact. Letters and donations poured in; nearly $60,000 was raised, much of it in small amounts. Children sent in their pocket money. More than enough was contributed to ensure the security of the project; indeed, questions are still raised today about what was actually done with all the money.

With the financial gap filled, Helen Yokoyama was on firmer ground in her subsequent refusal to allow any of the women to appear on television. She also decided that it had been a mistake to have any of them nominated as 'leaders' or 'spokeswomen' for the group. It would be much better, she thought, if they took it in turns to perform any small official function, to speak or answer for the group. She wanted them all, especially the shyest and least extrovert, to have the chance to open up, take responsibility and gain confidence in public. Again, this decision did not make her especially popular, but it was respected.

91

The day after the Hitzigs' reception, to Helen Yokoyama's relief, Ida Day took the whole party down to a Quaker retreat in the Pennsylvania countryside at Pendle Hill, where they stayed for two weeks of rest and preparation for the next stage of their trip. The women had coaching in English conversation, table manners, how to hold a knife and fork, and generally learned a little more about American customs; they were also protected from the press, who trailed them everywhere. Their arrival attracted wide attention, as the State Department had feared; but the prevailing note was more one of self-congratulation at American generosity than horror or guilt at the sight of scarred atomic bomb victims. 'Hiroshima Girls Here for Surgery: Most Impressed by Tall Buildings', said the *Herald Tribune*. 'They Voice Gratitude,' said the *New York Times*, 'Express Friendship for U.S and a Hatred for War – All Costs Being Donated.' Other headlines included 'US Opens Eyes, Heart to Hiroshima Victims' and, more crudely, 'Jap Girls to Get New Faces'.

Three days after the arrival, Norman Cousins sent a letter of appreciation and thanks to the General in charge of Mitchell Air Force Base, Long Island. Although undoubtedly true, it carried an ironic ring. 'The plain fact of the matter is,' he wrote, 'that this goodwill project between America and Japan would never have been possible without the US Air Force.'

While the party stayed quietly at Pendle Hill, Ida Day was busier than she had ever been, making detailed arrangements for the women to move to their host families. As with Dr Barsky, everyone with whom I discussed the Maidens project had nothing but good to say of Mrs Day. She seemed, to the Japanese especially, the embodiment of the Quaker virtues they found most admirable. The Japanese place great value on purity of

92

motive; the Quakers, who had nothing to gain from the
project, who avoided publicity about their role, whose
way of life was deliberately simple and unostentatious,
and who were genuinely grateful to have the chance to
express their love of God and their hatred of war in a
direct and human way, impressed them very much.

The Days had always lived in or near New York, and
Ida had worked in a Settlement House after leaving
college, teaching the violin. They both loved music,
sailing, dogs and children; neither was born into a
Quaker family; both had a social conscience which
eventually led them to become Quakers in the late
1930s, when they found themselves utterly opposed to
war, even a war to stop Hitler. Today, approaching
their eighties, they live in a small grey wooden house just
outside Old Saybrook on the Connecticut coast about
three hours from Manhattan.

They explained to me the structure of the Quaker
movement and how decisions about the Maidens were
taken. Quakers are strong believers in individual choice
and responsibility; so it was not a matter of New York
headquarters instructing local Meetings to ask for host
families, but of the proposal being sent to Meetings who
then discussed it and made their own decisions. The
Meetings were asked to consider taking responsibility
for two women for a year, who could perhaps be shared
between several families. Suitable homes would have to
have a comfortable spare room or maybe two, and the
mother of the family would need to be at home during
the day. The women would need to be taken to and
from Mount Sinai Hospital in Manhattan, and the
Meetings were asked to think how best to arrange
transport, perhaps organising a rota of volunteer driv-
ers. Host families were expected to look after the
Hiroshima Maidens as if they were their own daughters,
feed, clothe and provide for them in every way. They

were warned that the women might find an American diet difficult at first and that their English would be rudimentary.

According to the hosts I met, everyone involved was at first nervous about taking on such a responsibility. Although they were told that the women were all well-adjusted and healthy, they anticipated social and emotional problems. Nevertheless, twelve suburban Meetings in New York State, New Jersey and Connecticut decided that they would take up the proposal; two did so in conjunction with other churches in their neighbourhood. Each Meeting then made its own plans. Some found suitable hosts for most or all of the year, others soon had a list of several families and planned to move the women every month or two within the community. Wherever possible Japanese-speakers in the neighbourhood were asked to act as interpreters.

The couples who came forward to look after the Hiroshima Maidens were for the most part middle-aged or older, comfortably off, with good sized houses and, notwithstanding their Quaker beliefs, all the ordinary comforts of middle-class professional American living. Some had teenaged children, some had grandchildren. The affluent outer suburbs of New York in the mid-1950s during early summer must have struck the Japanese as the American dream come true. From the crowded streets of rebuilt Hiroshima, where most ordinary families slept in one room, the young women found themselves with their own rooms in rambling houses with modern kitchens and bathrooms, playrooms, garages, big gardens and swimming pools. They were treated with American openness and generosity by people who wanted to make up to them for some of the horror they had endured as a result of America's use of the atomic bomb. It is rare in Japan today for strangers to be invited into a Japanese home — partly because space is limited, partly for deeper reasons connected with privacy and dignity. In America, people instantly treat you as one of the family. The contrast is still striking; thirty years ago it must have been dramatic.

All the host families, I discovered, were relieved to find the women more cheerful than they had expected. Helen Yokoyama's advice to them, she told me, as they left for their new homes was to look people in the eye when addressed, to be themselves, and to behave, if in doubt, like 'good Japanese daughters'. She told them, and their hosts, that they should telephone her if a problem seemed intractable; she was on the phone a good deal during the first weeks. Most early misunderstandings occurred over food, or language, or a combination of both. One Maiden rang in tears, to say that although she had told her hostess she could not eat eggs, she was still being given them for breakfast every day; it turned out that when the American enquired, 'Don't you like eggs?' and the Japanese replied, 'Yes', she had meant to agree that she did not like them, but was understood to be saying that she did. Another Maiden, hearing her hosts call each other Honey and Sweetie, decided that these must be correct forms of address in American families. One hostess had the distinct impression that one of her guests was sleeping on the floor every night, although she always put the blankets carefully back on the bed.

All the Japanese women I spoke to recalled, among their first impressions, the amazing luxury of American life and the overwhelming kindness of their hosts. They also sensed very soon that although in America people might be shocked by their injuries, they did not attach to them the stigma felt in Japan. 'As soon as I arrived in America it was a warm welcome,' said Shigeko. 'I could feel it, like a vibration. In Japan people looked at me with pity in their eyes. Americans looked at me as if they wanted to be my friend. I don't say all America is like that; we were fortunate to step into a good group.' Michiyo was also amazed at the warmth she felt from her American 'parents'. She, and many of the other girls, were immediately asked to call their hosts mother and father. 'We were treated as kindly, with as much love or more, as they showed their own children,' she said, still sounding surprised thirty years later. 'We felt really cared for, and that we could say anything to them. It was like living in a dream world. Everything was so different and new. The dishwashers and the television and telephone! No Japanese like us could imagine living with such things in those days.'

Masako remembers that on her first night in Scarsdale, where she and Shigeko went together, their hosts took them out for dinner to a Japanese restaurant; it was much grander and more expensive than anything they were used to, and she was particularly impressed when they were told that they could order whatever they liked.

From the beginning, the women were showered with clothes, presents, taken on all kinds of outings, offered English classes, encouraged to pursue interests and hobbies. A report prepared by Ida Day a few weeks after they arrived gives some idea of the range of their activities and the efforts being made on their behalf. Two Maidens in Fairfield 'have visited the UN where their host works, made clothes for themselves, filled the house with their beautiful flower arrangements, and gone on shopping expeditions . . .' Two in Montclair 'have been attending the English class which the Plainfield Meeting arranged for the New Jersey girls, taught by Mr Shirato of Columbia, three times a week. Their hostess writes: "Our girls practice their English well at home and like my typewriter, sewing machine and piano . . . As both are good swimmers we hope for the kind of weather soon that makes our pool attractive to them again. In the meantime they've fixed their clothes, watched TV, baked cake and puddings and delved into a pile of magazines from Japan recently found for us." '

From Plainfield: 'The girls have gone sightseeing in New York, been taken up the Empire State Building and to a Japanese restaurant. Their hostess, who has a daughter of the same age and now considers that she has three daughters, wrote: "This is such a wonderful experience for us. Thank you for the opportunity." '
The women in Ridgewood had been making friends with a nearby Japanese war bride, and studying English from books given to them by a friend of their hosts. Others had a hostess who made pottery and was teaching the girls to use her kiln.

Ida Day concluded:

> Everyone who has entertained the girls has expressed deep affection for them and happiness in having them in their homes. There is unanimous agreement that the girls are the most considerate and endearing guests imaginable, always pleasant, responsive and thoughtful. Through force of necessity they are learning English very rapidly and learning to make themselves understood independently of the Japanese neighbours contacts which all the Meetings had made for them in their communities. All the girls needed clothing and in almost every case the hosts or Committees have provided what they lacked for the summer and feel that the Meetings will be able to meet the winter's needs . . . the Japanese American Association secured from the publisher in Japan a gift to each girl of dictionaries and phrase books . . . Many of the girls are learning typewriting, several piano, two rug weaving . . . Almost every family has asked us the same question: 'Did you know you were assigning us the two nicest girls?'

Clearly, all those concerned were on their best behaviour, and profoundly relieved at the initial success of the transition. One of the women, Toyoko, later gave me some indication that the picture was not invariably as rosy as it seemed.

'I don't think I could say we were happy at first,' she said carefully. 'They tried to speak to us but we couldn't understand. Then, if we wanted to do something we couldn't explain. Helen Yokoyama was not with us, and it was difficult to ask to make a telephone call to her. Our families were very kind, they tried to help us, and I'm sure they also had a hard time with us.' Then she laughed ruefully. 'I never ate tomatoes; I didn't like them. Every day they gave us tomatoes, but I didn't want to say I didn't like them. So I ate them . . . and now, I like them!'

9

Surgery

On 26 May, just over two weeks after they had arrived in New York, the first of the Hiroshima Maidens was operated on at Mount Sinai Hospital. Every few days for the next sixteen months, one of them would be on the operating table. The surgeons performed 127 operations on the twenty-five women. Dr Barsky was the senior surgeon, but he shared the work with his two younger colleagues, Dr Sidney Kahn and Dr Bernard Simon. During the first months, Dr Harada or Dr Ouchi assisted at the operations.

The hospital schedule lists a bewildering variety of technical terms connected with plastic surgery: 'Scar bridle', 'split skin graft', 'cicatrical ectropion of left lower eyelid', 'construction of abdominal tubed pedicle', 'defatting', 'Z-plasty'. The women had keloids removed, new eyebrows tattooed, and skin taken for grafting from their buttocks, stomachs, inner arms and thighs. One had a tendon transferred from a toe to a finger.

The Maidens were assigned to a room at the hospital; two of them were always there, either awaiting surgery or recovering. Helen Yokoyama, who stayed in Manhattan throughout the project, spent much of her time at the hospital, determined to be available to comfort the women in Japanese as they lost consciousness under the anaesthetic and when they came round. 'I would stand there holding their hand and saying over and over again, "It's all right, you're going to be all right," ' she said. 'It really was like being their mother.' Host families, friends and others connected with the project would visit the patients and bring them flowers and presents; one hostess, knowing the pain involved in skin grafts, arrived at the hospital one day offering to donate her own skin, not realising that only the patient's own skin will take. From the start, all the Americans were moved by the Japanese women's courage and cheerfulness. They were model patients. 'I was in the intensive care room when the first girl was brought back from surgery,' Ida Day told me. 'When she came round, the first words she said were in English; she said, "Thank you, Dr Barsky."'

Dr Bernard Simon is still practising; I went to see him at his consulting rooms just off Park Avenue. He was the youngest of the surgeons involved and is now the only surviving member of the team. Dr Simon is a small, dapper man in his seventies who likes to talk about his work and arranged to see me as soon as he knew that I was interested in the Hiroshima Maidens project. 'This is a labour of love!' he said, sounding emotional. 'This is something very, very dear to my heart. I represent not just myself, but two very wonderful people now deceased.' On the wall of this office I noticed two large prints of Japanese warriors, and two framed certificates elaborately decorated, in Japanese. They were tributes from the medical community and the city of Hiroshima. I turned one over; it gave the English on the back:

In cooperation with Dr Barsky you have participated in the project to give medical aid to the Hiroshima Maidens suffering from the effects of the bombing, and have conducted surgical operations with utmost care and thoughtfulness for a long period of eighteen months despite your loss of time and resources, and your brilliant achievement has secured a bright prospect of life for the Maidens.

His office is pleasantly cluttered with easy chairs and a sofa, embroidered cushions, many family pictures, portraits, photographs of his mentors and colleagues, drawings by some of his child patients and many shelves of medical journals and books on plastic surgery. He took one down to show me; it was a fat textbook entitled *The Principles and Practice of Plastic Surgery*, by Arthur Barsky, Sidney Kahn and Bernard E. Simon, published by McGraw Hill in 1964 and reprinted many times. The frontispiece shows a series of small coloured photographs of injured faces in various stages of repair, including one of a Japanese woman. 'Yes, that's one of the Maidens,' said Dr Simon. 'Of course it's all terribly out of date today.'

Dr Simon spoke with great warmth about the Hiroshima Maidens project, with which he was evidently proud to have been associated. He was especially eager to tell me how impressed he had been by Helen Yokoyama, whom he described as a 'brilliant, extraordinary human being', and by Ida Day and the Society of Friends. He referred to the Maidens as 'a loving, grateful, wonderful bunch of kids'.

He told me something of his background. 'You could say I've had a chequered career,' he began. 'I was kicked out of school for anti-war activity, and then spent four and a half years in the armed services.' He had been at Columbia Medical School in the mid-1930s, and became involved in student agitation. 'Just as now young people are disturbed by the prospect of nuclear war, so we were disturbed by the prospect of war itself,' he explained. 'There were anti-war strikes throughout the university. My view, and my friends', was that we would not bear arms except in defence of our country. But of course the moment there was that incredibly brutal attack on Pearl Harbor, all bets were off.' In the meantime he was expelled from Columbia, but managed

101

to be accepted at Johns Hopkins, where he qualified as a surgeon in 1937.

During the war, his pacifist inclinations put aside, he served in a medical unit attached to front-line troops. Had he, like Norman Cousins and the Quakers, felt that America was wrong to drop the atomic bombs on Japan? Dr Simon bristled. 'On the contrary!' he said. 'It's a decision that everyone would have taken. It appeared to be an endless war. We knew that Japan was having difficulty, but we also knew that when you actually invade a man's homeland he's going to fight to the last. I was in a camp in southern France waiting to join in the final assault on Japan when the bomb fell, and we were all most grateful because none of us expected ever to come back. It was figured that a million Japanese would die and our casualties would be about 250,000.' So he had not felt any special responsibility towards the Maidens he operated on, as representatives of the survivors of Hiroshima? 'No, not at all,' he said firmly. 'As a matter of fact I was a little ... er ... disturbed. At that point I was kind of neutral. They were our patients, it had to be done, and I felt the compassion one would feel for any patients who had been hurt. The point was that there were so many people who emphasised our guilt, and I had none!'

Had he been surprised by the nature of the scarring? 'They were pretty much what we expected. A great mistake was made by some of the press and the public; these were not burns caused by the gamma radiation, that knocks out bone marrow. These were pure flash burns, burns of a high intensity from exposure to extreme heat for a short period of time.'

There were two special problems, he conceded. 'We knew the Japanese had a tendency, somewhat like the blacks, to grow thicker scars, keloids. But keloid is not a function of pigmented skin; it's genetic. Asian and

African people are somewhat more prone to develop thickened scars, that's all. And the Japanese — I don't have to labour the point that they are among the most brilliant people in the world, but with all their cleverness the one medical specialty that they did not have at that time was plastic surgery. These kids had had a certain number of attempts to skin graft them but the efforts had been somewhat inadequate, and all it had really done was to wreck certain donor sites.'

I asked Dr Simon to explain some of the surgical techniques used on the women. What, for instance, was a tubed pedicle, which seemed from the list he had given me to play an important part in reconstructing some of the most badly damaged faces? 'Well, it's not much used any more these days,' he said. 'What you do is, you take an extra fold of skin, usually from the abdomen; you make two vertical incisions, perhaps ten or twelve inches long, and then you cut it away from the flesh underneath, so you now have a loose strip of skin, attached at both ends. You sew it around to itself to make a tube, and then you stretch and close up the skin underneath it.'

He showed me some pictures of patients looking like a version of the Elephant Man, with tubes of their own skin and flesh attached to their arms, legs or faces. The next stage, he explained, is to detach one end of the tube and re-attach it either to where the graft is needed or, more usually when the skin from the stomach is intended to repair the face, to a place halfway between the donor site and the scarred area. The purpose of this is to maintain the circulation of blood in the skin; when the tube from the stomach has established itself satisfactorily on, say, the arm, it is then cut again and re-attached to the face.

What this meant for the several Hiroshima Maidens who needed it was a series of three or four operations, each leaving painful wounds. While each stage was healing they had to lie completely still. 'It's a very tedious procedure,' said Dr Simon. 'It means operation after operation, over several weeks. Nowadays, what we usually do is to take a free flap, a piece of skin say from the groin with an artery and veins, and attach it directly to the site with microsurgery, joining it to another artery and veins. A number of techniques have developed since then that we would use today.'

If you have to use skin from the stomach on the face, or the hands, as they did with several of the Hiroshima Maidens including Shigeko, Toyoko and Hiroko, you then usually have to perform the defatting procedure. 'The skin on the stomach is plumper than skin else-where,' explained Dr Simon. 'In order to preserve the circulation you don't take the fat off at first . . . once the circulation is established you lift up one edge of the graft and trim a good deal of the fat away from underneath.'

The other operation performed many times was the comparatively simple procedure called a Z-plasty. This was used to loosen tight scar tissue which had con-tracted to form webs, holding the arms or fingers rigidly, or pulling the chin into the neck. 'It's a simple matter of transposing triangles,' explained Dr Simon, showing me another picture. 'You break the straight line by cutting a series of zig-zags, which then stretch out and act like an accordion.'

Everyone was concerned that the women should not expect miracles from the American surgeons. Dr Barsky especially went to great pains to explain to them that while excellent results could be expected where it was a matter of restoring functions, any improvement to their appearance would be a long, slow business. There were, however, some dramatic moments during their treat-ment. One came after Terue, whose left eye had been open and weeping for ten years, had three operations on her eyelids. She kept a diary describing what happened. On 8 June 1955, Dr Simon took a patch of skin from the inside of her right upper arm, and grafted it to her lower eyelid; on 23 November he did the same for the upper lid, taking skin from her left arm. He sutured her eyelids together, so that the new lids would not contract while the grafts healed. On 16 February 1956 she wrote in her diary: 'The doctors said they were going to open my eye today. Many people came to my room, including Dr Simon and Dr Barsky. I was filled with excitement but I was also frightened.' Dr Simon cut the sutures apart, and then told her to open and shut her eye.

'I opened my eye timidly. It saw light for the first time in eight months. Then I closed my eye slowly. It shut firmly. Yes, on its own. I asked the doctor, "May I look in the mirror?" He said, "Yes, all right." I took a hand mirror out of my bag. I blinked over and over again. I could close my left eye for the first time in ten years. Could I be dreaming? Tears of gratitude streamed down my cheeks.

'Dr Simon asked, "Are you happy?" Sobbing in sheer joy, I impulsively gripped his hands. I said to him, "Yes, doctor, I am very happy. I shall never forget you, never." As long as I live I shall never forget these intense feelings. How good it is to be alive.'

Helen Yokoyama remembers that the most moving moment, for her, was when Hiroko T., after twelve operations including the tubed pedicle method to bring skin from her stomach to her face, was at last able to open her mouth properly. Helen asked her what she would most like to eat: Hiroko wrote down on a piece of paper: 'A hot dog.' Helen went out into the street and bought one; she gave it to Hiroko, who managed for the first time to open her mouth wide enough to take a

full-sized bite. Both women were in tears. Helen remembers that Dr Barsky, standing by, wept too.

As the months passed, it began to seem to some of
those observing the Hiroshima patients that changes
were taking place in the women that had nothing
directly to do with surgery. All the warmth, generosity
and attention being lavished on them by their host
families, the treats and the spoiling and the new oppor-
tunities, were having a noticeable effect. Despite all the
anxiety and pain, their morale improved; they became
more confident and outgoing.

To Dr Simon, who had been struck by how scared
and miserable the girls had looked as they got off the
plane, the alteration in their appearance and state of
mind within a few months was gratifying. 'After we did
the first three or four operations word went out around
the group that we were not going to hurt them, and that
they were being treated in the hospital with loving
kindness,' he said. 'Meanwhile, Ida Day and the Friends
were doing more for the girls than all the surgery we did.
They were not treated like pariahs any more; after all,
they were used to being told to stay in the back room
and sleep on the ashes in the kitchen, like Cinderella.
Suddenly everybody adored them, they were wined and
dined, people gave parties for them.' It seemed as if the
more the Hiroshima Maidens took on the style and
attitudes of young Americans, the more satisfied their
hosts felt. 'By Christmas their awful perms had grown
out; it was the time of the Italian cut, so there they were
with their blue-black hair straight and smooth; their
families had given them cashmere sweaters and plaid
skirts and flat shoes like American college girls. Suddenly they blossomed, as people.'

Several times, when the women were due to move on
from one household to another, Ida Day was telephoned
by the host family and asked whether they couldn't stay

longer; the American 'parents' were finding their guests not only easier than they had expected, but good company. 'Believe me,' said Dr Simon earnestly, 'as a surgeon of forty-seven years' experience I can tell you that there are things in the soul and heart that are more important than the body. You can release eyelids, but there are still scars from the skin grafts; you are more comfortable and you look better, but you are still scarred ... to me the psychological aspects of the Hiroshima Maidens project were the most exciting thing about it.'

It was clear to me, talking to the Americans connected with the project, that the responsiveness and cheerfulness of the women made them feel better about themselves and their country. Instead of resentment and fear, the Hiroshima Maidens showed them trust and affection; the emotional impact was very great. I wondered if the women themselves would recall the way they were said to have blossomed in America, and how it had struck the other Japanese attached to the project.

Certainly, all the women I later spoke to confirmed Dr Simon's opinion. In Japan, I felt, their scars had set them apart from other people, except for their immediate families; people were sorry for them, but they tried to avoid contact. The scars were a constant reminder of a national trauma. In America, people they met were concerned about their scars, but not repelled. Being good to individual Maidens gave them a welcome chance to exorcise their feelings of guilt towards all the victims of the atomic bombings. For the women, the simple fact that they were treated with ordinary warmth was the most tremendous relief. 'Americans are so open,' said Toyoko, whose friend in Tokyo had warned her not to go for fear of being treated as a freak. 'There, I felt just like everybody else; sometimes I even forgot that I had scars. I think all the other girls will say the

same thing.' Helen Yokoyama has always remembered
something that another of the Maidens said to her as she
was wheeled into the operating theatre: 'Tell Dr Barsky
not to be worried because he cannot give me a new face.
I know this is impossible, but it does not matter.
Something has already healed here inside.'

Dr Tomin Harada, who had had reservations about
joining the project, and who still felt sensitive to the
imputation that American surgeons were succeeding
where Japanese had failed, was also impressed with how
much the Americans were doing for the Maidens in
other ways. He described a visit he made to one family,
where Michiko S., the girl whose face he had found so
appalling when he first saw her, was staying. Her hosts,
Edward and Vesta Miller, lived in Ridgewood, New
Jersey, but had taken Michiko to their holiday cabin in
the woods for a few days. The Millers were in their
fifties; he was an executive with a New York telephone
company. As Dr Harada arrived at the cabin, he heard
voices and women's laughter; when he saw Michiko, he
saw that some of the laughter came from her.

'I was startled,' writes Dr Harada. 'I hadn't seen
Michiko for two months. This was the first time that I
had ever seen her laugh. She had seemed to be a girl who
had forgotten how to laugh, a girl with a frozen face.'

The Millers had nicknamed Michiko 'Mickey', and
teased her and made jokes with her. 'Frankly, I was
puzzled,' says Dr Harada. 'Those muscles that control
facial expressions, which had seemed lost in the hard
keloids, had suddenly begun to function. And this was
not after ten operations; Michiko hadn't even had her
first one since coming to America.' He asked the Millers
what sort of magic they had been using.

Edward Miller said: 'Other than exercising a little
special care because of the language difference we
haven't done anything at all. We've merely tried to take

her into our lives completely. We were surprised too at the way that she opened herself up to us. I guess she must have been wanting to do that for a long time, but for some reason just wasn't able to before.' Thinking about it afterwards, Dr Harada thought he could understand. In Japan, he realised, people treated Michiko with curiosity, or pity. The Millers treated her with ordinary, casual affection.

For all the remarkable success of the relationship between the Hiroshima Maidens and their host families, there were, inevitably, some awkward moments. Neither side finds this easy to admit; I was struck by the evident need, even thirty years later, for everyone concerned to present only the best image: the Americans as models of openness and warmth, the ideal surrogate Western parents, and the Japanese dutiful, lively and grateful, the model Oriental daughters. At the time there was also a genuine fear that if anything went publicly wrong, the whole project might fail; difficulties were therefore handled with the utmost discretion, which has persisted to this day.

Not all the women, I gathered, got on well together, which was hardly surprising given the wide age span (between seventeen and thirty), the range of backgrounds and education, and the status-conscious nature of Japanese society. Helen Yokoyama was well aware of the precise social gradations in the group, of who was from a 'good family' and who was not, and she tried to protect the more vulnerable and to encourage the superior to behave with American lack of class-consciousness. One of the group, she knew, came from Hiroshima's 'floating world', the entertainment quarter of bars and brothels; she would see this Maiden, who in fact behaved, as Helen said, 'like a perfect Japanese girl', so that none of the Americans had any idea of her past, gaze wistfully into bars and dance halls in New York as they went on well-organised group outings. Some of the others were not very nice to her and she felt, Helen knew, that they looked down on her. Another woman had been in trouble with the police in Japan for shoplifting. Ida and her hostess kept a close eye on her, and if she was late back from the city — for the Maidens were soon confident enough to take the bus or subway in and out of Manhattan by themselves — Ida would check the hospital, or the other places the group would meet, and take her home. One of the women became badly homesick and depressed; there was talk of sending her back to Japan, but everyone felt it would damage the reputation of the project to do so. Instead, Helen Yokoyama took charge of her until she recovered.

Helen's determined protectiveness led to the occasional confrontation. Some of the women thought she fussed too much, as did one or two of the Americans. Helen was adamant, for instance, that the group should not be examined or interviewed by psychiatrists, as was suggested by some of the American doctors, who felt that their emotional needs should be examined as well as their physical problems. Psychiatry was unusual and still suspect in Japan at that time, and she thought the Maidens were too vulnerable and too unsophisticated to deal with it. She also feared that there would be an outcry if any such thing leaked out in Hiroshima. There were further battles over publicity; on one occasion, Dr Hitzig became furious with Helen when she refused to let two of the women appear on a television programme and arranged for two of the hostesses to substitute for them.

On the tenth anniversary of the bombing of Hiroshima, 6 August 1955, Helen Yokoyama spoke on behalf of the Maidens to the New York press. 'It is something they want to forget,' she said. 'They are less self-conscious here; they have grown more self-assured.

They feel that the United States is a wonderful place, a dreamland. Yet they say that no matter how poor Japan is they want to go home as soon as their treatment is over. They feel strange that they should have survived, and they feel that for this they owe something to the world.'

In Hiroshima, the anniversary was celebrated by the First World Conference against Atomic and Hydrogen Bombs; a few weeks earlier, Bertrand Russell and Albert Einstein had launched a peace campaign in London. At the end of August, the Peace Memorial Museum was opened in Hiroshima. The same week, in New York, the first big news story, with pictures, about the operations in progress at Mount Sinai Hospital appeared in the New York *World Telegram*. 'Surgeons Knife Battling A-Bomb', said the headline; 'Decade of Hiding Coming to End For Hiroshima Maids in Project Sponsored by American Citizens'.

Although most of the accounts of the Maidens' progress appearing in Japan were also positive, in September 1955 a critical note was struck. Dr Masao Tsuzuki, the eminent director of the Red Cross Hospital in Tokyo and Japan's leading expert on radiation effects, visited New York and went to Mount Sinai to see how the girls were getting on. Afterwards, he expressed his reservations. Interviewed by a Japanese correspondent in New York, he told the Tokyo press that he felt the results of the operations so far were 'not optimistic' and that 'for the goodwill of both nations this should be the only and last time that A-Girls be sent to the United States for surgical treatment . . . Viewed from a surgical standpoint, it is clear that there are some unsatisfactory factors because the attempt was made without adequate preparatory knowledge.' He cited the tendency of Japanese skin to form thicker scars, the unfamiliarity with keloid formation of American

111

surgeons, and the special nature of thermal burns. He feared, he said, that when the girls returned to Japan 'it might be said that after all the publicity the results are not so good.' Reading between the lines, it is clear that Dr Tsuzuki was anxious to defend the reputation of Japanese medicine. 'We do not believe', he went on, 'that plastic surgery in Japan is so behind that of the United States.'

He also wanted to ensure that the project did not distract the attention of both countries from the needs of atomic bomb survivors in general, which urgently needed to be tackled. 'The A-girls are but a small part of the many suffering from A-bomb effects and we must not forget that there are many who are yet critically ill. The deeper understanding created by the girls welcomed in American homes is the greatest benefit achieved from this project. But if I were to be consulted on any such project in the future, I will clearly answer, "opposed".'

Two days later Norman Cousins' answer to Dr Tsuzuki appeared in the same paper. His tone was as always diplomatic, but carried an edge of irritation. 'The girls are free of the many misconceptions about plastic surgery that apparently exist in relation to this project in both the United States and Japan,' he said. When pressed by the reporter about whether he considered American surgeons better than Japanese, his reply was crisp. 'We didn't bring them over here with any idea of doing it better. We brought them because it wasn't being done at all.'

For the most part, however, the project progressed smoothly, with Maidens and hosts deriving much pleasure and satisfaction from their encounters. Ellen Cousins remembers giving several big reunion parties at the big house in Connecticut where they then lived; she had invited Shigeko to stay with them and they made preparations for the parties together. 'She was very outgoing and loving,' says Mrs Cousins. 'She and I had a wonderful relationship from the start. I always wanted her to stay with us. When she first arrived she had dozens of little bandages all over her, and she didn't seem to me to be healing very well. I kept on finding these little bloody bandages all over the house. I've always been very strong on good nutrition, so I put her on a special diet, and she healed up fast. Our youngest daughter was five or six and they had a lovely relationship too; she became a member of our family. She was bright. Norman taught her to play chess before she could speak English.' For the parties, they put up a yellow and white marquee on the lawn, and Ellen Cousins and Shigeko would work for three or four days preparing food. 'We would make brown rice, chilli con carne, chicken teriyaki, a big fruit salad,' said Ellen Cousins, 'and maybe a hundred people would come. Everyone would play games afterwards; the girls were always all over Norman, and he always knew their names and everything about them.'

The Hitzig family gave a big summer party too; this time it was to celebrate the eighteenth birthday and impending departure to Somerville College, Oxford, of another of their daughters, Cayla. A home movie survives of this party, showing the Hiroshima Maidens smiling and relaxed, running over the grass and swimming in the pool; they dressed Cayla Hitzig in a Japanese kimono with flowers in her hair, and she gave each of them a present. Sometimes the women would give their hosts a treat, cooking a Japanese meal, making a dress or a quilt. Ida Day remembers such an occasion: 'They were so sweet, every one of them. They all had keys to our home in Forest Hills, which is on the subway, and as time went on they would go into New York and do things and we never knew who might turn up to stay the night. On my birthday I was surprised by

113

all the girls saying, "Happy Birthday!" – they had prepared a birthday dinner for me.' Deborah and Robert Teel, who had Michiyo living with them for a while, were delighted when she took up painting; they entered one of her watercolours in a local art sale and when it was sold for $15 she touched them by saying that she was sending the money to Mount Sinai Hospital.

Early in 1956, Helen Yokoyama relaxed her guard enough to allow several of the girls to be interviewed, and photographed, for a series of articles in the *New York Daily Mirror*. 'America can drop the biggest bomb,' stated the paper proudly, 'but it can also make the biggest, warmest gesture of goodwill.'

10

'Just a Stupid Accident'

On 24 May 1956, just over a year after her arrival in the United States, Tomoko Nakabayashi, one of the least badly injured of the Hiroshima Maidens, had her third operation at Mount Sinai. She had already had surgery on her right arm, to release the tight scars that had held her elbow at an awkward angle, and skin grafts to the arm and right hand; this was to be her last operation, and it was one that both she and the surgeons had considered marginal. A keloid remained on her right upper arm, and she decided in the end that she would like it removed. Dr Bernard Simon did the last operation, as he had done the first two.

The record he showed me conveys the basic facts. 'Excision of scars of right upper arm: split thickness skin graft: cardiac arrest and resuscitation. To recovery room and death five hours later.' Tomoko's heart stopped under the anaesthetic. The team worked frantically to revive her, but in vain. She was twenty-six, and had taught dressmaking in Hiroshima; she was planning to stay on in America to study hat design. 'She was a peach,' said Ida Day, 'a real peach. I blame myself; I encouraged her to have the last scar removed.'

Dr Simon recalled the tragedy all too vividly. 'It was the most terrible thing, and the worst part was that it was just a stupid accident,' he said. When Dr Simon realised that something had gone wrong he started resuscitation procedures; soon the whole hospital knew what was going on. 'None of the staff went off duty that night,' said Helen Yokoyama, who as always was present when one of the Maidens was having an operation. 'They couldn't have done more if it had been the President's life in danger.' Norman Cousins was summoned; Dr Hitzig and Dr Barsky were already there. 'Norman Cousins was distraught, and Dr Hitzig was in tears,' said Helen, conveying, despite her American education, a characteristically Japanese amazement that men, especially men in a position of authority, could let their emotions show in public. She found herself trying to comfort Dr Hitzig. 'I put my arm round him – of course he was much bigger than me – and said, "Now, now, Dr Hitzig, now now . . ." '

The Americans felt an appalled responsibility that a woman who had endured the atomic bombing, survived, and then trusted them enough to accept treatment should die under their care. They were terrified of the impact her death would have on the other Maidens and on public opinion in Japan. They feared that the party would demand to be flown home immediately and that the whole project would collapse in recriminations. While they tried to think how best to handle the tragedy, messages were sent to Tomoko's parents and the Mayor of Hiroshima; Dr Harada, who by this time had returned home, was asked to try to help contain the situation. Meanwhile Helen Yokoyama had to tell the other women what had happened, and assess their feelings.

I didn't tell them what to do; you don't always have to, you know. I just said to them: what you girls can do at this time to show your gratitude for what has been done for you here is to be calm, and to show trust and respect for the doctors. Then I called up the girl who was due to be operated on next. I said, 'Now, Misako-san, you know what has happened, that there has been a tragedy. You are

116

scheduled to come into the hospital next. You don't have to come if you don't want to.' She was furious. 'What do you think I am?' she said. 'I'm going to leave right away!' I met her at the elevator in the hospital; she was carrying her case. She glared at me, she really glared, and then she stamped off to her room, in true American teenager style.

Later, Helen Yokoyama went to a crisis meeting at Norman Cousins' office. 'They just didn't know what to do,' she said. Afterwards, Cousins took her back to the hospital in his car. 'On the way, he stopped; he put his head down on the wheel and sobbed, actually sobbed. "Oh Helen, has it all come to nothing?" he asked me. I just said to him, "Mr Cousins, let's go and see the girls." There were two girls in our room in the hospital, and as soon as they saw him they smiled. "Don't worry, Mr Cousins," they said. "Everything will be all right." '

Everyone, including Helen herself, was amazed by the Hiroshima Maidens' reaction. There was no panic; instead they tried to cheer everyone else up. Helen Yokoyama had originally planned to go home to Japan after six months but had decided to stay on; her husband, she told me, had asked her how she would feel if anything went wrong with the Maidens after her departure. 'I thank God that I was there, that I had stayed,' says Helen Yokoyama seriously; and it seemed to me that her dual loyalty to America and to Japan and her instinct for self-control must have been vital. 'I didn't cry,' she said, when she told me about it. 'Not one tear, until everything was settled. Then, when I was alone, I just had to bawl.' She was impressed when, at another special meeting, Dr Hitzig apologised publicly to her for some hard things he had said about her in the early days of the project when they clashed over

117

publicity. He knew that without her steadying influence over the group the reaction to Tomoko's death might have been very different.

In the Cousins files there are several items relating to Tomoko's death. Among them is a note from one of the Maidens, dated three days afterwards, addressed to 'Our dear doctors and Mr Cousins'. It reads: 'Doctors you please always remmber [*sic*] that we all believe in you and we wish to cooperate with this project until and after we go back in Japan. Yours sincerely, Tadako (for all of the Hiroshima Girls)'. He also kept a copy of the message he sent to Tomoko's parents: 'She was much beloved by everyone who knew her. Our grief is boundless. Her American family joins me in sending condolences.' Also in the files is the message that, to his immense relief, came back from Hiroshima. 'We sincerely hope that this unexpected misfortune will not discourage you and your greatly humanitarian plan which has been conducted very successfully. We still have every confidence and hope for you. Respectfully yours, the parents of Hiroshima Girls.'

In Japan, the news did not provoke a general outcry against the project or America, although Tomoko's brother was quoted as saying that he felt the Americans had killed her twice. The main question raised was whether her death was in any way related to radiation or after-effects of the atomic bomb. When it was explained that there was no connection, and Dr Harada addressed a meeting in Hiroshima, described the dangers of anaesthetics and reassured the public that everything possible had been done to save her, the matter was allowed to rest. 'The response from Tomoko's mother was most touching,' said Dr Harada later. 'She said: "The atomic bombing claimed so many lives. But my daughter was allowed to go on living happily – even though for a short while – among many generous people. It wasn't the surgery that killed her; the war killed her. I must accept this reality." '

Even so, Cousins blamed himself. He remembered how he had chosen to disregard warnings about possible risks and failures. 'I can't get away from the feeling that something I initiated led to what happened,' he wrote to a friend. Shigeko remembers his distress. 'He was taking me home from the hospital to his house two weeks later. On the way, we stopped at a park, and went for a walk. He was not talking, I think he is thinking about Tomoko. So I say to him, look at the flowers! After the winter, the spring always come! So then he smiled, and we went to a café to eat lunch before we go home. I knew Mrs Cousins was expecting us home for lunch, so I was surprised; but when we get there and I tell her we already eaten, she was pleased, not at all upset. Later she tell me that since Tomoko died, he hardly eat.' Recently, Cousins recalled the incident. 'I felt a measure of personal responsibility for that tragedy . . . When the unthinkable happened, I wondered whether I had been pigheaded in going ahead. I have a tendency to put a perhaps unreasonable amount of faith in positive approaches and I wondered whether this trait was responsible for what happened to Tomoko . . . It hung over me for many years.'

On 31 May a requiem mass was held for Tomoko in New York; she had been the only Catholic in the group. About a thousand people were there, including all the host families and friends, and the Mount Sinai team. Tomoko's hostess from Montclair, New Jersey, spoke in praise of her qualities and said how much they had loved her. There was another mass in Montclair and the Quakers held a service of their own. A week after she died, the operations resumed. One of the women wrote to Ida Day: 'I heard from Helen that your very sad please don't sad I know Tomoko she don't like sad. She likes every body happy. She is paradise now please don't worry any more.'

Two weeks after the memorial service for Tomoko, nine of the Hiroshima Maidens returned to Japan. The other fifteen still had operations to come; they were to stay another few months. There was a round of goodbye parties; Dr Hitzig arranged a day out for the girls and their American families, including a boat trip round Manhattan, dinner at a restaurant, and a night baseball game between the Giants and the Dodgers. The Days took them to the opera. The Quakers gave a big reception for 300 people at the Meeting House in New York, where several host parents spoke about how valuable an experience it had been. When the Maidens said goodbye to the Mount Sinai staff, each one was given a photograph of the hospital, a book describing its origins and history and – at their own request, as a souvenir – a towel bearing the hospital's name. On 15 June the nine women, each with a red flower in her lapel, gathered at Idlewild airport for the first stage of the flight, again in a US Air Force plane. Dr Takahashi, who had replaced Dr Harada, was returning with them. He carried Tomoko's ashes in an urn wrapped in a white cloth.

Several of the American host parents were in tears as they hugged the departing Maidens; the Maidens wept too. 'I was excited to be going home, of course,' says Terue, 'but it was very painful to say goodbye to so many wonderful people and not know if we would ever see them again.' Ida Day came to the airport with her own battered typewriter, and gave it to Terue as a farewell present. She has it still.

When they arrived at Tokyo, the party left the plane for breakfast and a press conference. The first person to descend the steps was Dr Takahashi, carrying the urn.

The group faced the reporters and photographers from behind a long table, with the urn, garlanded with a wreath, standing in front of them. Its presence made the mood of the return subdued; one radio station reported: 'The scars don't look much different from the time when the girls left; all looked gloomy and evaded questions by the press.'

At Hiroshima, the Mayor and other city, church, and medical officials were lined up to meet them as well as their families. The parents of the dead girl were also present. Again, Dr Takahashi led the party off the plane. He handed Tomoko's ashes first to the Mayor of Hiroshima, who then gave them to her father. One of the women made a short statement: 'As friends we are very sorry about the loss of Miss Nakabayashi. We are stricken with sorrow and loneliness, but we really don't know what to do. For a long year we were warmly cared for in America not as Japanese but like their own daughters. In daily life and in medical treatment the Americans treated us as if we were their own children. We are really grateful.' She also thanked the Mayor and the reception committee. After the Mayor had spoken and a Catholic priest had offered prayers, the girls were able to greet their families.

According to the *Nippon Times* reporter, who had accompanied the group to the United States, 'There was a smile on each face and cries of "welcome home" were heard from the ground. True to Japanese mores, however, there was no hugging among kinsfolk.' He went on to say that of course everyone was looking at the women and wondering how much improvement had been made to their appearance. 'To the casual observer,' he wrote, 'the superficial improvement was not necessarily impressive. Unless he had a vivid memory of the scars the girls had before leaving for New York last year, he might not see much difference on the faces, which were

121

still far from normal.' The Mayor of Hiroshima, however, thought otherwise, as he said in a letter to Norman Cousins:

> It was my impression that the girls looked far better in every way than they did a year ago. As they stepped down from the plane I immediately noticed that they no longer felt embarrassed to meet the people. The consensus of the parents was that their daughters came back even better than they had expected ... Let me again assure you that nothing can ever bring collapse to this project, and nothing can deprive it of the vast spiritual importance that no one with an honest heart could ever fail to see.

Before going home the Maidens were taken to another memorial service at the Peace Park. As they stood by the Cenotaph in the rain, an American reporter heard a young male voice shout: 'Do you think you are the only ones scarred?'

By the end of September, the Mount Sinai team had completed the operations on the fifteen remaining girls. Helen Yokoyama and Ida Day wanted to show them something more of America than they had so far seen; so they travelled to California by bus, looking at Williamsburg, the Grand Canyon, the Rockies and Disneyland before they reached Los Angeles, where they were entertained by the Japanese community, and visited Hollywood. In San Francisco they were joined by Norman Cousins, and Dr Barsky and Dr Simon, who were to accompany them back to Hiroshima; some of their American families crossed the continent to see them off. In the end, only thirteen of them flew back to Japan. Toyoko had decided to stay on and study dress design at Parsons School in New York. When it turned out that her treatment was going to take longer than the anticipated six months, she had had to drop out of the course she had been taking in Tokyo. 'I think maybe I cried,' she said. 'At first I wanted to go back to Tokyo, but everyone said no, you can't go back now, the doctors say you can't go yet. Mrs Day said, why don't you go to design school in New York? At first I didn't want to because my English was still very poor, and my mother was not happy when I asked her. But Mrs Day said I could stay with her, and so I said I would, just for one year.' And while the group was in California, another girl decided to stay on with some Japanese-American relations.

This time, Cousins had persuaded Pan American to give the group a complimentary flight. He described in the *Saturday Review* the cheerful scene on the plane: 'From where I sit in the rear of the cabin I can survey the entire party. I can hardly believe my eyes, for two rows of seats have been converted into a hairdressing establishment.' One of the Maidens had trained as a hairdresser and beautician in America, and was returning with enough capital, raised by the community in which she had lived, to start a small beauty parlour. She spent most of the flight doing her friends' hair. Several of the Maidens had typewriters with them and were hoping to get secretarial jobs. Shigeko, according to Cousins, had decided to study nursing. When the women started taking out their passports to fill in immigration forms, one of them 'let out an astonished squeal. "It is someone else," she said. "They will never let me in again." '

Despite such encouraging remarks, Cousins and the surgeons knew that the women's faces would be scrutinised and that some people would find the results disappointing. On their way through the airport at Hawaii, a stranger had approached the party and asked in hushed tones if nothing could be done for their faces with plastic surgery. The Americans winced, but said nothing. What they all did feel able to rely on was the Maidens' new confidence and capacity to deal with life. In Tokyo, at a big lunch given for the party at the Foreign Correspondents Club, it was Michiyo's turn to speak on behalf of the group. She had been so shy eighteen months before, Cousins recalled, that she would only whisper. Now, although visibly shaking as she rose to speak, she made a clear, strong speech in English. 'I hold out my arm to you,' she said. 'This is not a simple thing. It means much to me to be able to do this. For many years my arm was bent tight like this [she folded it in to her side and then straightened it out] – this is what you see; what you do not see is the heart that is so full.'

Everyone connected with the project knew that it would not be easy for the women to settle back into life in Hiroshima. Helen Yokoyama had been worried about it from the start. The Maidens had discussed the problem with her and Ida Day and among themselves. But they were full of their new confidence and their plans and sure of support, financial and moral, from the American friends they had left behind. Even so, one of them said something ominous to a reporter soon after her return: 'In a way I envy Nakabayashi-san. Oh to be loved, to win a scholarship, and then to die without facing the problems of coming home.'

Part 3

Japan and America, 1956–85

11

Aftermath in Hiroshima

The Hiroshima Maidens project had raised hopes that were not going to be easy to satisfy, and the women themselves soon found that their position as symbols of these hopes and promises was not easy either. Among those most eagerly awaiting the return of the second group, particularly when it was known that Dr Barsky and Norman Cousins were accompanying them, were the eighteen who had been interviewed but not selected. On several occasions, Cousins had been quoted in the Japanese press as saying that he regarded the treatment of the original twenty-five as just a first step, and that he and everyone concerned with the project knew that much more had to be done for the many other victims of the atomic bombing. Remembering earlier promises, the eighteen felt sure that this time they would be at the head of the queue and that they too would be going to the United States for treatment. There were rumours that next it would be the turn of the boys and young men who had been injured as schoolchildren; and that enough money had been raised, through the Reverend Tanimoto's appeal on 'This Is Your Life', to finance this.

Although most of the publicity the Maidens received on their return was friendly, some was not. One Tokyo paper wrote: 'Many of the Hiroshima Maidens who recently returned from plastic surgery treatment in the United States have been spoiled by the experience . . . Back in their own drab houses, the girls are beginning to realise that the rude awakening from a beautiful dream is a bit hard to take.' The girls were criticised for their smart, Americanised clothes, and for the amount of make-up they wore; this seemed especially hard, several of them told me, as they needed make-up to conceal their scars and had been excited to find a range of special creams made by a Miss O'Leary in New York, who had undertaken to supply their needs free of charge. It seemed that if they looked subdued and let their scars show, the press claimed that the project had failed; if they looked happy and confident, they were accused of being spoiled. They managed to joke about it; one day a newspaper carried pictures of the returning Maidens beside a photograph of the newly-crowned Miss Japan. 'Well, anyway, I'm Miss Pikadon,' said one.

Someone who could not help her feelings of hope and envy was Miyoko, one of the eighteen rejected girls. She had followed the progress of the others in America: 'I was all the time working with the blind children,' she told me. 'The others sent me letters they were having nice time with host families; I cried.' And when they came back, was she impressed by the improvement? 'I didn't feel jealousy for their operations,' she said quickly. 'They didn't become well; you could still see scars. But when they came back they wore beautiful clothes; in Japan we were still poor. We never saw such colourful clothes, and they looked very cheerful.'

Two days after arriving in Hiroshima, Norman Cousins, Dr Barsky and Ida Day went to a special meeting at the Reverend Tanimoto's church, where several of the returning Maidens got up to talk about their experiences. Among those present to hear them was Miyoko; she addressed the meeting too. 'It is such a wonderful world you have been telling us about,' she said. 'Ever since you left we have been reading your letters and talking to your families. The wonderful pictures would grow and grow. And our prayers each night got larger too. We prayed so loud we were certain the Americans would hear us across the oceans and cause our dream to become true. Now we look at the beautiful new dresses and coats of the girls who have come back and we see new lights in their faces and we wonder if these things will ever happen to us.'

In fact, it had already been decided that the Hiroshima Maidens project was to be the first and last attempt to treat atomic bomb victims by taking them to the United States. The Americans and the Japanese agreed that although the idea had worked out on the whole remarkably well, it was not practical to think of a repetition. To give special treatment to one symbolic group was justified not only in terms of the benefits to a handful of individuals, but as an exercise designed to draw attention to the horrors of nuclear war and to put pressure on both governments to take the problems of all *hibakusha* seriously. However it was not an approach that could work with large numbers, either in America or Japan. The *Japan Times* pointed out after the return of the first group in June 1956 that 'The Japanese government is spending this year approximately $75,000 for all treatment of Atomic victims in both Hiroshima and Nagasaki. This is roughly equivalent to only one fifth of the amount spent on the 25 girls who went to New York.' Dr Takahashi, the surgeon who had brought back Tomoko's ashes, told a reporter: 'The surgical treatment received by the girls in New York is not beyond the skill of Japanese doctors, but the cost and social situation prevailing now would make undertaking of the project difficult in Japan.'

The day after the meeting at the Reverend Tanimoto's church, Cousins and the others had the delicate job of telling Miyoko that she would not after all be going to the United States. First they went to see the home for

129

blind children where she worked, a small, dingy building near the centre of the city. Miyoko demonstrated how she had taught the children to play games and to bow to distinguished guests. She also showed the visitors the new braille typewriter that one of her former workmates, Masako, had brought back from the USA. 'The tour of inspection over, we went downstairs for the frank talk with Miyoko,' wrote Cousins. They told her that the medical and other reasons that had prevented them from taking her and the others still stood; but, 'we had all come back to assure the Eighteen that we now had the means to provide for their treatment within the city itself.' Dr Harada would make the arrangements, and the funds were already there. They also promised that Quaker families would be found to adopt her at a distance, provide her with vocational training, and send her clothes and presents. They asked her to tell the other seventeen girls that the same would be done for them.

At the time, Miyoko took it well, according to Cousins. 'She replied that this was more than she wanted or felt she deserved. She had gone to bed the night before with a heavy heart after returning from the Reverend Tanimoto's church, because she had allowed herself to be carried away by wonderful visions; but she understood that some things were not to be.' Thirty years later, however, she told me that it was only after she had formed a close relationship of her own with an American woman in the peace movement, who took her to the United States, that she stopped feeling bitter disappointment.

The Cousins party had another, even more difficult, visit to make: a condolence call on the parents of the girl who had died. The Nakabayashis received the Americans with a dignity that profoundly impressed them. The small, modest house had cloths pinned up to hide cracks in the walls; in the main room stood a shrine to their dead daughter, with candles burning in front of one of the last pictures of her, taken by her American host family. They expressed their thanks to the Americans for all the joy Tomoko had experienced in their country; then they presented them with two elaborately carved models of Spanish galleons that they had made by hand. Mr Nakabayashi was in poor health; he had had a stroke, and wept as he talked. His wife apologised for his tears, which she said were tears of gratitude, not grief. Like Miyoko, the Nakabayashis achieved in front of Cousins and the others a superb demonstration of the Japanese capacity to control unacceptable emotions in public.

The Americans then had a round of meetings with the Mayor, his officials, and the medical establishment of Hiroshima. They wanted to know how they might best continue to help care for bomb victims. Dr Harada explained that since the foundation of the Atomic Bomb Patients Treatment Council in 1953, just over 15,000 people had presented themselves for medical care. In mid-1956, he estimated, 1,575 of them needed urgent treatment, 931 for radiation-related illnesses of an internal kind and 644 for plastic surgery. He suggested that the Americans could help by contributing money, and also by sending surgeons and other specialists to work with the Hiroshima hospitals. It would also be a good idea, he thought, if Japanese surgeons could spend regular terms in America to gain experience. Cousins promised to do what he could.

At the end of a week the American party left Hiroshima. Over the next few years, some of the hopes and promises created by the Hiroshima Maidens project were fulfilled, but others were not. The eighteen women who had been left behind were not, so far as I could discover, given any special help. According to Miyoko, some of them received treatment in Hiroshima, but not at American expense; and she did not recall that they were put in touch with Quaker families. It seemed to me that once the prospect of living for a time in America was removed, the eighteen became resigned to making the best of their situation without relying on American help. Dr Harada was vague about what became of the plans discussed with Cousins for continuing support for bomb victims: 'I believe that he very probably wanted to help the eighteen and other *hibakusha*, but to my knowledge he didn't make any firm promises, nor did he take steps to do anything further,' he told me. 'He did once ask me if the Maidens needed more money, but I told him that they had already received much help . . . His project did help *hibakusha*, indirectly, by arousing Japanese public consciousness that saving *hibakusha* was really Japan's responsibility.'

In 1957, partly as a result of the publicity generated by the project, a Society of Plastic Surgery was established in Tokyo, thus giving this specialism professional standing for the first time. For several years thereafter, young Japanese plastic surgeons went to Mount Sinai Hospital in New York to gain experience. One of them later wrote the first plastic surgery textbook in Japanese, superseding the standard work by Dr Barsky and his colleagues.

Also in 1957, the Japanese government passed the first of a series of laws providing free medical treatment for A-Bomb victims. This was a landmark in the bleak story of the *hibakusha*, and it is generally agreed that the Hiroshima Maidens project helped to bring it about.

During the 1960s, although pressure to obtain further medical and financial aid for *hibakusha* continued, campaigners in Hiroshima found themselves drawn into the wider movement of protest against nuclear tests and stockpiling of weapons by the Great Powers. Survivors from the bombings of Hiroshima and Nagasaki were often called upon to play a part in these campaigns, and at first some did; but increasingly, as quarrels and splits divided the Japanese peace movement, mainly between Communists and non-Communists over whether the Soviet Union as well as the Western powers should be criticised for the arms build-up, *hibakusha* found themselves bewildered and alienated. It seemed to them as if the factions were more interested in the struggle for dominance than in preventing nuclear war.

Meanwhile, the twenty-two women who had returned from America in 1956 had to work out how to live the rest of their lives.

12

The Risk of Marriage

For many of the Maidens the daunting question now arose, since their scars were less disabling and their morale better, of whether they could, or should, get married. There is no subject more delicate, frightening and complex than whether or not people exposed to the atomic bomb and the effects of radiation are likely to produce deformed children. Most of us are instinctively surprised to learn that people badly injured in the bombings have survived to live anything like normal lives. We are even more amazed to learn that women such as the Hiroshima Maidens could have normal babies. Yet thirteen out of the twenty-four women married, and nine of them produced a total of nineteen children, several of whom now have children of their own.

To date, although the effects of the bomb on fertility and its genetic consequences have been minutely studied, there is no evidence of any statistically significant impact. Experts admit they find this puzzling; from experiments with irradiated animals they would expect genetic damage to occur in humans. One theory, not universally accepted, is that those who survived and reproduced were those who were least susceptible to radiation; a crude form of survival of the fittest. So far, *hibakusha* have married and reproduced roughly in line with their unexposed contemporaries. There is no evidence up till now that survivors have had fewer children, or that more of their children have had something wrong with them. However, all the experts agree that no final conclusion about the ultimate genetic consequences of the atomic bombings can yet be drawn.

These trends are, of course, clear only with hindsight; and this is not to say that fears about damage to reproductive systems and genetic damage were or are unfounded. They arose first of all because immediately after the bombing, many pregnant women miscarried and there were other noticeable effects on the female system. Over 70 per cent of women in one survey in Hiroshima had menstrual disorders afterwards; the incidence of abnormal menstruation correlated with distance from the hypocentre. Those worst affected by radiation sickness had the worst problems. For most women, these disorders cleared up after about a year; nearly 80 per cent of the women surveyed in Hiroshima were apparently back to normal by March 1946. But by that time, one of the most horrible and alarming of the bomb's after-effects was becoming clear; among babies who had been foetuses in their mothers' wombs at the time of the bombing, there was a marked increase in microcephaly (an abnormally small head) and associated mental retardation. It was only natural, in the circumstances, for any miscarriage or stillbirth or baby born imperfect in Hiroshima to be ascribed to the bomb, and for women survivors to fear the consequences of becoming pregnant.

There were other special problems for women *hibakusha* which it is known now were either temporary or not serious but which at the time must have caused much anxiety and speculation. Women approaching the menopause at the time of the bombing experienced it somewhat earlier than the average; and it was observed that girls approaching puberty did not start menstruating until twelve to eighteen months later than average. Most of the Hiroshima Maidens fall into this latter category, and one of the doctors involved in their treatment told me that several of them had experienced menstrual irregularities for a while. However, the medical check-ups they were given before being taken to the United States ruled out any serious problems of this kind.

Statistics and check-ups notwithstanding, there is no doubt that most *hibakusha* felt, and many still feel, recurrent, intense anxiety about the possibility that their children, grandchildren and even great-grandchildren might, even if born healthy, develop problems in time as a result of the bombing. No one can be quite sure that the full extent of its effects has been discovered; research is still going on. Nothing impressed me more than the courage of the women I met who had taken the risk of marrying and having babies, or moved me more than meeting or being shown photographs of their children and grandchildren.

The first of the Maidens to marry was Mitsuko, the girl who surprised everyone by staying on in California with her Japanese-American relatives. She subsequently married one of her cousins. The next was the youngest woman in the group, Yoshie, who had been writing secretly to a boyfriend she had known before she left for America. They were married ten days after she returned: when a journalist asked the new husband whether he thought that Yoshie had come back looking prettier than when she left Hiroshima, he answered: 'I always thought she was pretty.' Within the next two or three years, several more of the girls married, including Michiko, whose face had once horrified Dr Harada, and Terue, whose eye had been repaired by Dr Simon.

For Terue, the decision to marry was not easy. She had schooled herself so firmly for so long not to think about love or marriage that even with her scars very much improved and new, positive feelings about life it was hard to change. When I said that this conflict must have been hard for her, she gave me a reproving look: 'Hard is too mild a word,' she said. 'It was like denying myself a basic human right.'

She had known a young man who had also survived the bombing, but escaped without external injuries, before she went to America; he lived in her neighbourhood. While she was away, he translated some letters written by her American hosts to her father; he was studying English at the YMCA. He began writing to her himself. 'Then my American family thought he was my boyfriend,' she said, 'but I always told them he was not.' All the same, I wondered, did she not start secretly hoping, that he might be? Again the look of mild reproof. 'Not at all. It never even occurred to me.'

She went to dressmaking school, but started to see something of her young neighbour as well. 'Our relationship developed gradually and naturally,' she said. 'First we were just ordinary friends. When I did begin to think about marriage, I still thought it was impossible. I was afraid of radiation sickness and what could happen if we had children.' The young man was determined to marry her, even though his family was against it; they would much have preferred him to find someone who had not been in the bombing. It was widely thought that to produce children when both parents had been exposed to radiation was bound to be more risky than if only one had. 'I suffered a great deal,' she said. 'There were many rumours about babies being born deformed.' But Doctor Harada reassured her that the risks were small, and her future husband never wavered. 'He was really steadfast and sincere,' she said. 'He helped me to make up my mind, and after three years I said yes.' Another person who backed her up was Helen Yokoyama. Many of the women continued to rely on her for advice and support. 'I introduced him to

Yokoyama-san; she told me she felt she and I could trust this man,' said Terue.

As Terue looks back, she feels that it was her time in America, both the success of her operations and the confidence she gained from her American families, that transformed her attitude towards life. Her appearance and her self-esteem, both damaged by the bomb, had been restored. 'That's why I was able to take the risk of marrying, and why I am as I am today,' she told me firmly, taking a small photograph album out of her bag and showing me pictures of her two daughters, her son, and their families; she has three grandchildren.

When she was first married, did she feel worried that she might not be able to have a normal baby? 'I was always afraid; that fear never went away,' she said, calmly. 'Even today, with my children and grandchildren, I feel it, that something might go wrong with them. They tell me I shouldn't worry like this; but they are a different generation, how can they know? They never had the experience I did.'

For all her recurrent fears, it was impossible not to feel, meeting Terue, that she had made a remarkable breakthrough into normal life, the kind of life as a wife, mother and grandmother that she would always have chosen. Another of the Maidens, Hiroko, has a very different story. She made a marriage as extraordinary as Terue's sounds ordinary, although both seemed to me in their way heroic.

Hiroko T. was the girl who first saw herself, after the bomb fell, in the bowl of a spoon, whose scars were so bad that she wore a mask, and who wept when her mouth was finally opened wide enough for her to be able to bite a hot dog. Her face was always one of the most disfigured of all the girls, and despite the many operations she had in New York (she was known as 'The Champ' because she had more than anyone else) it

138

is still a shock to look at. The whole of the lower part of her face, from just below the eyes, is grossly distorted. Her nose is a twisted lump; her lips are shapeless and protruding. Under her chin is a thick mass of corded scars running down her neck. Her cheeks and chin and jaw, from ear to ear, are curiously puffy-looking, the skin stretched very tight and unnaturally plump and smooth, while around the eyes and on the forehead it is fine and dry and now slightly wrinkled. At first, it is hard to look squarely at Hiroko. Soon, however, her own apparent unselfconsciousness makes embarrassment irrelevant; and I found, as with the other badly scarred women I met, that very soon, certainly within half an hour of meeting them and starting to talk, I stopped seeing the scars at all.

Hiroko is a quick-witted woman who laughs readily and appears to be completely without self-pity. She told me how she first met her husband, Harry, an American ex-marine ten years older than she is, who retired not long ago from the *Baltimore Sun*, the Maryland newspaper where he worked for many years as a packer and driver.

'He read an article about the Hiroshima Maidens in the newspaper. My name was there, and he wrote to me at Pendle Hill. Then he came to see me in the hospital, and brought me flowers.'

Harry, it turned out, had a younger brother whose face had been badly injured by a bomb during the war against the Japanese in the Philippines; his nose was blown off, but he had been greatly helped by plastic surgery. This, and strong Catholic beliefs, made Harry determined to do anything he could for Hiroko; soon he was pressing her to marry him. He told Helen Yokoyama he wanted to make Hiroko happy. At first Hiroko was suspicious and half-angry; she had never liked people feeling sorry for her. 'What he think he is, I say?' she told me. 'No one can *give* me happy life! I had my own dreams for my life. If I had been a beautiful woman, Miss Universe, I could understand him, but . . .' Helen Yokoyama and the Mount Sinai doctors were uneasy at first, too. 'When I first met Harry he asked me which of the girls had the severest scars,' Helen has said. 'I thought of him as a very odd fellow . . . But there was no mistake about his devotion to Hiroko.' She decided that the only thing to do was to let Hiroko make up her own mind.

It took Hiroko ten years, during which time Harry never stopped writing to her and pressing her. After she returned to Japan, she studied dressmaking, worked in Tokyo for a while, opened her own shop in Hiroshima and became a dressmaking instructor. 'I did all the things I had wanted to do,' she said. 'Now I think maybe because he keep asking me like that, it gave me courage. If somebody love you, you feel not bad! He keep on saying he can make me happy; so I think, maybe I can give him some happiness too.' Again, she went to Dr Harada and Helen Yokoyama for advice; they both encouraged her, saying that Harry's steadfastness had impressed them and if she wanted to marry him she should go ahead. They were married in Baltimore in 1965; among the guests at the wedding were the families who had been her hosts in America ten years before. Her wedding dress was a present from her dressmaking teacher in Hiroshima.

Until three years ago they lived in or near Baltimore. Harry continued to work for the *Sun*, and Hiroko found a good job in a department store, selling women's fashions. When Harry retired, they decided to return to Japan and live with Hiroko's mother at her old home on the small island in the Inland Sea. It is about three hours by boat and train from Hiroshima; they come into the city regularly, for Hiroko to attend an art class and to

140

see Dr Harada, who has continued to treat Hiroko. She had needed several more operations in the past years; there is a keloid on her throat that keeps coming back. Dr Harada told me it was the most persistent scar growth he had known.

Hiroko's attitude to her disfigured face is matter of fact, and humorous. 'Like when you tear your dress, patches is patches,' she said. She has had twenty-nine operations in all, and should probably have more; her mouth, which was opened by Dr Barsky at Mount Sinai, is now too tight again, and she could have more work done to remove the fat deposits which are the cause of her lower face looking unnaturally smooth and puffy. 'This is my stomach skin, that's why getting too fat,' she said, putting her small, pretty, unscarred hands to her cheeks and laughing. 'But I don't like to trouble any more.' She is more bothered by her right arm, where she has arthritis in the elbow, and her left arm is still stiff; it was burned to the bone, she explained.

Her matter-of-fact attitude to her injuries astonished me. Had she never felt near despair? She looked at me and smiled. 'So many of the others said they thought about killing themselves: I, never! I never think seriously about it. If I think back on my life, I think I was really a lucky girl.'

13

Jobs and Jealousies

Most of the women returned from America determined that, whether they married or not, they would find jobs. In several cases, they had acquired new skills or qualifications; all of them had been encouraged by their American friends to make something of their lives. The publicity they received in Japan on their return helped them get started; businessmen and local government officials in Hiroshima made special efforts to find them work. Again, this caused some jealousy; other survivors saw them once again as being given an unfair advantage. All of them who wanted to found work quickly at first. One went to work in a hotel; two were secretaries in local government; one became a telephone operator. Michiyo, who had run from her office to be interviewed, found that her old job was waiting for her. Several of them went back to dressmaking. One went to work at an old people's home. Suzue opened her beauty parlour with capital raised by her American hosts; soon she was helping other scarred women disguise their disfigurement.

Toyoko, who had stayed on in New York to study fashion design, and live with the Day family, could never quite resign herself to remaining unmarried; but she did find her studies more and more enjoyable. She, more than any of the other women, seemed for a time to have achieved professional and financial success. At the Parsons School, she settled in fast with the other students although she was ten years older than most of them, and, according to Ida Day, who came to love her dearly, showed real talent. 'I loved the students and the teachers,' says Toyoko now. 'At first I was not so sure, but then I said yes, this is the kind of school I want.' The American kids called her Tommy and seemed genuinely not to notice her scars. 'Sometimes I even forgot I had scars, because nobody ask me about them,' she said, sounding wistful. During her second year, she went to Europe for six months with the school, toured England, France, Germany and Italy, studying art and architecture. At the end of her third year she graduated with honours, top of her class. Some of her drawings were published in the *New York Times* and she was offered jobs designing or teaching. But she was determined, she says, to go back to Japan and make her career there. She also wanted to help the other Hiroshima Maidens, if she could. 'Some of the girls had written to me saying they would like to start a dressmaking business,' she says. 'So I decided to come back.'

She returned to Japan in the summer of 1959, full of plans and backed with money and orders from her American friends. Ida Day and some other hostesses helped to arrange orders; she designed them dresses, obtained silk from Japan and fitted them individually. 'There were over one hundred dresses to be finished here and sent back,' she recalled. She set up her own small business in Tokyo, with the help of two other Maidens, one of them Hiroko; her dream was to give work to as many women from Hiroshima as she could, whether or not they had been members of the group.

At first all went well. Six women from Hiroshima came to Tokyo and they began to prepare a fashion show to launch the enterprise. Then Ida Day decided to come to Tokyo herself to help Toyoko: she arrived with a French friend, Germaine Aubry, who proved to be a valuable contact; she was well connected, and had introductions to French and other diplomats. Ida Day remembers with delight the way her French friend dealt with the manager of the Imperial Hotel, the grandest in Tokyo at the time, where they hoped to put on the fashion show. 'I had already been to explain to him what we were trying to do and to ask if we could have a corner of the lobby,' she said. 'He just looked at me in a superior way and said, "Madame, we are a commercial operation, not a charity." Then Germaine went back and told him about the people she was going to invite, and of course he couldn't do enough for us after that.'

The venture was launched at a lunch for two hundred at the Imperial Hotel, on 7 October 1960. There was a large group from Hiroshima present, including the other Maidens, the Mayor and Toyoko's mother, whom Ida Day had arranged to bring up as a surprise. 'It was a secret; and then we sat her next to the Mayor and gave her a big bunch of flowers,' Ida told me. 'There she was, this little bent old lady who had never been anywhere before, who had worked as a cleaner most of her life. It was wonderful.' Ida herself announced the show in English, wearing a dress made for her by Toyoko. There were five models, nineteen dresses, and much applause. It was widely reported in the press: 'Hiroshima Maid Makes Tokyo Bow as Style Designer, Warmly Praised', went one headline. It was emphasised that all six assistants were victims of the bomb, and that Toyoko hoped to give employment to many more. She was quoted as saying: 'To devote my life to a job will be the best way for me to forget the horrors of nuclear weapons.' Over thirty years later, Toyoko remembered the occasion with evident pleasure and pride. 'It was really exciting,' she said. 'I think in my life, it was the glorious time.'

The enterprise indeed seemed to be a great success, a wonderful climax to the whole Hiroshima Maidens project, with Toyoko putting her American experience and support to the best possible use, fulfilling her own talent and helping her friends. The business expanded until ten women were working for her. One of the Maidens brought her younger sister from Hiroshima to help in the workroom part-time and study in Tokyo. But Toyoko began to run into financial difficulties, and she also became aware that some of the Hiroshima women disliked taking orders from her. As she talked of this unhappy period, Toyoko became visibly upset. 'I did assume the leadership,' she said, 'but not because I wanted to be in command. I wanted us all to be like sisters, with no superior or inferior. But in business, someone has to be the boss; and I think this aroused resentment.' When she started to hire extra help, in Tokyo, the Hiroshima group became still more discontented. Money was a problem, as they thought that Toyoko should pay them more than she felt the business could afford. 'I was not good businesswoman,' said Toyoko, trying to laugh but wiping her eyes. 'I loved the fun of doing it, not so much the business.' She tried for a while getting one of the other Maidens to pass on her instructions, but this did not work either. When she ran into serious debt, the Days helped her for a time with the interest on her loans. Gradually, the other Hiroshima women left; Toyoko felt she had been deserted. 'It was a very awkward situation. I felt I wasn't liked any more.'

Eventually she had to reorganise the business so that it was much smaller, with a few clients with whom she could deal individually. She also found extra work as a teacher and consultant. She had assumed that she would stay permanently in Tokyo, but about ten years ago she started to have problems with her health and decided to return to Hiroshima, where she has a sister and other family nearby. For all the happy memories of the start of her designing business, it is an awkward subject among

145

the Maidens and their friends. Some feel Toyoko was let down; others, that she exploited the group for publicity and tried to make a success at their expense, turning a project intended by her American backers to benefit them all into an enterprise of her own.

As I learned more about the difficulties and disappointments encountered by some of the group after they returned to Japan, both from outsiders and among themselves, I found myself often relating their experiences to the American psychiatrist Robert Jay Lifton's unique study of survivors of Hiroshima, *Death in Life*. The book is based on research conducted in the early 1960s; but its delineation of the predicament of *hibakusha* is timeless. Lifton had spent nearly four years working in Japan on a study of Japanese youth before he began to investigate Hiroshima. His particular interest has always been the relationship between individual psychology and historical change, and how the human psyche deals with extreme experiences; when he began to investigate the possibility of compiling a study of *hibakusha*, he discovered that there had been no detailed or systematic study of the general social or psychological effects of the bomb. This was partly because Japan remained suspicious of the psychiatric approach for a long time; indeed, there is still a strong emphasis there on the physical origins of mental disturbance. It also reflected, he suggested, the 'emotional impediments' felt by everyone who approached the subject.

Lifton's book is based on interviews with about seventy-five survivors, men and women, over a wide range of ages and occupations. He presents *hibakusha* as engaged in an intense struggle to resolve their feelings about themselves and the terrible event they have experienced, which he sees as an extraordinary and unique 'immersion in death'. Among the psychic consequences he detected were a pervasive guilt at having survived when so many died, and at not having been able to save or help others; profound and lasting fear and shame, especially about being contaminated by radiation or marked by keloid scars; and deep ambivalence towards the receipt of special help or attention, no matter how well-meaning. This ambivalence Lifton calls 'suspicion of counterfeit nurturance' and what he means by this daunting phrase seems to me to be especially enlightening when applied to the experiences of the Hiroshima Maidens.

Survivors of the atomic bombings are likely to be caught in a vicious circle. Their ordeal left them with special problems and needs; but any recognition of those needs has been felt to be confirmation of the damages they had sustained, and so reinforced their deepest anxieties and fears. The effect of this dilemma has been to make *hibakusha*, both as individuals and as a community, highly sensitive and touchy, especially about offers of help from outsiders. They need help, but they are suspicious of it, and especially suspicious of those among them who accept it. 'No one acquainted with Hiroshima life can fail to note the intensity of jealousies and resentments felt by *hibakusha* toward one another, especially toward those who step forward and take some kind of initiative,' says Lifton.

Accepting help and support from Americans was particularly complicated emotionally and psychologically. The Hiroshima Maidens were seen in some quarters as symbols of Japanese weakness and dependency: injured young girls being handed over to the victorious enemy. But despite these painful complexities, Lifton also discerned a deep need in *hibakusha* to be reconciled to individual Americans; and he found a corresponding need among Americans themselves: 'a hunger on both sides for an intimacy that would dissolve persisting

147

psychological discomforts surrounding the bomb.'

I went to talk to Dr Lifton in New York about some of the issues raised in his book and by the Hiroshima Maidens project. He is a tall, rumpled man in his late fifties whose most recent academic post has been as a Professor of Psychiatry at Yale. Since his work on Hiroshima he has continued to investigate human responses to extreme experiences; he has looked at survivors of Nazi concentration camps and worked with participants in the Vietnam war. He has been much involved in the American activist Left and has demonstrated and spoken out repeatedly against militarism and nuclear escalation. His wife, Betty Jean Lifton, is a photographer who has also worked in Hiroshima.

'I know some of the Maidens suffered on returning to Hiroshima,' he said. 'They were representative of Hiroshima in a very extreme way, although the same sort of thing happened to anyone who was singled out for special treatment. One of the problems of being a *hibakusha* is that it is very hard to find a target for your anger: so people turn on each other.' He reminded me too that the Japanese traditionally not only disapprove of anyone who stands out from the rest, they make every effort to bring them back into line; the phrase commonly used is 'hammering down the nail'. He also pointed out that the Maidens' journey to America and back can be seen as part of a complex pattern which began in the late nineteenth century after Japan was opened up to the West, whereby the transformation of Japanese society, inevitably in some ways a painful process, was undertaken by people who had made a similar journey. 'The people at home often reacted against the process of change,' he said. 'They used to say that the Japanese who came home full of new ideas smelled different; they 'smelled of butter', which to a Japanese is not a compliment. The Maidens in particular would have discovered

148

different kinds of relationships in America; then when they came back, some of them probably felt a reaction against change even in themselves.'

Had the Americans involved, I wondered, underestimated the sensitivity of the Japanese? 'Well, with something like this, anything one does is going to touch a raw nerve,' said Lifton. 'How can you make reparation to people who have been through an atomic bombing? There's no way.' He felt, though, that the project was significant partly as one of the rare attempts by Americans to break out of what he has called 'psychic numbing', the inability to think or feel, one of the most common responses to the facts and implications of what happened at Hiroshima. As a result, the emotional release on both sides during the project was intense, and such strong feelings can be hard to handle afterwards.

Another theme of Lifton's struck me as relevant to the Maidens' experiences: because of the scale of the devastation at Hiroshima, the amount of suffering and the number of deaths, survivors tended to be hard on themselves if they showed ordinary human weakness or selfishness. Their duty to the dead imposed high standards on them; it was as if they had to earn their reprieve from death by being noble and strong. Other people, especially foreigners, often shared these unrealistic expectations: 'Outsiders, like *hibakusha* themselves, bring to Hiroshima demands for purity that cannot be met,' says Lifton. The people of Hiroshima have always been particularly critical of anything that could be seen as exploitation of their experience for commercial purposes. They called it 'selling the bomb' and were contemptuous of any such activity. Toyoko's dress design business, I thought, must have suffered as a result.

All the same, Lifton saw in the Hiroshima Maidens project an example of one of the few ways in which *hibakusha* could be helped to recover their emotional well-being. The experience of being loved and welcomed in America had a positive effect on them, separately and also as a group on whom much public attention was focused.

It seemed to me that in the light of Lifton's findings the emphasis placed so heavily by both the Japanese and the Americans I spoke to on the spiritual or emotional benefits of the Hiroshima Maidens project became more understandable. Cynics have suggested that the psychological rewards of the venture were stressed because the physical results varied; it was safer to enthuse about something that could not be seen and evaluated objectively. But I concluded that their American experiences had indeed, at the time and for some of them long afterwards, helped the Maidens' morale and self-esteem. They had been singled out and made to feel loved and appreciated. Several of them said to me that in the years that followed, when times were hard, they would think of their time in America and of all the people who had shown they cared about them and as a result felt better able to cope. In his book Lifton sums it up: 'For individual *hibakusha* the experience of being loved and cared for could gradually, and against obstacles, re-create life-affirming imagery and re-establish the capacity to live.'

14

Shigeko in Manhattan Beach

All the women I met had, in their different ways, remade their lives after the project was officially over, except one. For the rest of them, the time in America receded as new phases in their lives developed; but for one, Shigeko, the Hiroshima Maidens project somehow became a permanent way of life. Within six months of her return in November 1956 she went back to the United States and she has lived there ever since. I met her in Los Angeles, where she has lived since 1978; and partly because with her there was little or no language barrier, partly because of her nature, which is uninhibited, we were able to talk very freely.

During her time in America she had decided she wanted to be a nurse, and just as the Days had encouraged Toyoko to live with them while she finished her design course, so Shigeko expected to live with the Cousins family and do her nurse's training. The Cousins were really fond of Shigeko, but wanted her to see her family before any decision was made: there had also been some jealousy within the group at Shigeko seeming to be the Cousins' favourite, and it was thought better not to confirm this impression by leaving her behind. But Shigeko was quite determined, and the group's mixed reception in Hiroshima did nothing to discourage her. She asked Norman Cousins to sponsor her return to the United States as a nursing student, and he agreed. Since then, her relationship with the Cousins family has been central to her life; she considers herself, and is considered by them, as part of the family, by '*de facto* adoption' as Cousins puts it.

Shigeko qualified as a nursing assistant; she then worked for a time looking after the well-known *Life* photographer Margaret Bourke White, who was suffering from Parkinson's disease. Meanwhile, she had become seriously involved with a young Japanese whom she had first met while she was in New York for treatment and he was a student. 'We met at the Japanese Church in New York City,' she says, 'and then again at one of the tea parties given for us. All the girls were around him; I paid no attention.' Three or four years later, in the early 1960s, when she was back and living with the Cousins in Connecticut, they met again. 'We got married,' she says. 'But the marriage ended after six months when he had to go back to Japan.' Shigeko was already pregnant; she had a son in 1963, whose first two names are Norman Cousins. Shigeko, who is unusually frank and open on personal matters, absolutely declines to talk about the failure of this relationship. 'Some people say we were never married, I know,' she told me. 'I can't stand that kind of gossip! It's my life! I think it's unnecessary for people to know other people's problems. I feel lucky! I met a wonderful man; then we found we could not make our life together. But I got a wonderful son; I have no regret. This is how life is. I accept.'

Because she has lived in America now for nearly thirty years, Shigeko's way of life, and her whole perspective on the past, is very different from that of any of the other Hiroshima Maidens I met. She has, over the years, cut loose from most of the patterns and expectations of the group she decided to leave behind, although she is still in close touch with her remaining family in Japan. In the process, she has become in some ways more confident than the other women and in others more vulnerable. Shigeko has, as Cousins told me, an endearing personality, a childlike spontaneity of trust and affection; within moments of meeting her, you feel charmed by her and protective towards her. At the same time she shows considerable strength and resilience, which she must have needed; her life has had an erratic, almost bohemian, drifting quality which seems to suit her well enough but which must also lead to anxieties. Her anchors are her love for her son Norman, and her attachment to the Cousins family.

I spent a day with Shigeko in Los Angeles, where she and Norman now live. They were about to move house when I was there; they had been living in a small, modest rented bungalow near the sea at Manhattan Beach, some way across town from the Cousins' hilltop house. We spent part of the day driving around the city, taking a message to Norman at his law school, visiting a Japanese shopping centre, having lunch in a Chinese restaurant. Shigeko drives a battered old car with great aplomb; she is a small woman, and the steering-wheel seemed a size too big for her, but she grasped it firmly with her small, scarred hands and hunched forward, talking eagerly, as we raced along the six-lane freeways.

'At first, when I come to America, Mr Cousins to me was like a god,' she said cheerfully, 'I shake!' She bowed low over the steering-wheel and gave a dramatic tremble. 'I feel very very humble. Then one day Andrea, one of the Cousins' daughters, say to me, "Don't worship Daddy! He's *not* God!" So then he become like a father instead.' Had she felt from the beginning that there was something special about her relationship with the Cousins, I asked? 'Norman Cousins everybody's friend,' she said quickly. 'All the girls jump all over him and love him. But me, maybe, I don't know — perhaps I was more helpless emotionally, or mentally. I was very naïve and immature; all the other girls were very quiet and

153

ladylike; me, I run around like a child. Sometimes when we all go to Cousins house, Mr Cousins pull me down to sit beside him, like a little girl.'

When she decided to return to America, and to live with the Cousins, how did the other girls feel, I wondered? And her parents? 'Mr Cousins wrote to the girls that I was going back to stay with them. Then I feel them cold to me; I feel I am an outsider. One girl in Hiroshima, not part of our group, where I worked for a while looking after children when we got back, she was very jealous, very nasty to me. But I pay no attention. Somehow, I think, my life just arrange itself. My father, at that time, was not very well. He just say – I cannot be sure to look after Shigeko; I will not take this opportunity away from her.'

Soon after she returned to America, Shigeko started to be active as an anti-nuclear campaigner. Whenever she was asked to support a peace rally, or address a meeting or tell a journalist of her experiences at Hiroshima, she would agree. Gradually she has become more committed; she is now much involved with a group called Physicians for Social Responsibility started by peace activists within the medical profession. At the same time, however, she feels very strongly that it is a mistake for *hibakusha* to turn their experience of the bomb into the determining event in their lives. Over lunch, she explained to me how she feels.

'I don't like us to be categorised just as victims,' she said fiercely. 'Of course we are in a unique position; the atom bomb was unique. But human life is very complicated for everybody; OK, because of the atomic bomb we have some special difficulties, but if we let our feelings about it get all mixed up with everything else, it makes life even harder.'

Did she mean, I asked, that some survivors tended to blame everything that ever went wrong in their lives on the bomb? 'That's right. People blame the bomb if they get sick, or no one will give them a job. Other people have trouble finding work too, and other people get cancer! I'm not saying we can forget what happened to us; look at me, you can see my face, my hands. But I want to use this experience – not for me, for others.'

She had been shocked, she told me, by the attitude of some of the Hiroshima survivors living in California who, when asked to help campaign against nuclear weapons, had said they did not want to risk annoying the American government at a time when they were appealing for special allowances from them. 'They are *using* being atomic bomb survivors, using it as an excuse!' she said, sounding really angry. 'No excuse! *You* cannot say it, but *I* can. We have to live life strong to help this world; we are in important position! We have to cope with other problems in our life. I think I was fortunate to survive, and that now I can help people who never had a war experience, so it never happen again. That's the only time I can use this weapon! I don't mix up being a survivor with my whole life! Many other people do; that's why so miserable!'

Did she not share, I wondered, any of the fears felt by the other women about their health, especially as they grew older? And had she not been anxious, when pregnant, about the possibility of her baby being abnormal?

'No,' she said very firmly. 'When I was at nursing school, I saw many babies, so many, with something wrong. Nothing to do with bomb! So I just pray: God, please give me healthy, good baby.' Her son is now twenty-two. How did he feel, I wondered, about what had happened to her? 'He never talks very much about it now,' said Shigeko, 'but I know he care about me. I remember one day when he was seven or eight I heard a schoolfriend ask him – "What happened to your

155

mother's face?" And Norman said: "You stupid! I told you not to mention it! I told you what happened! My mummy is lucky: she didn't die". Now, I think he still want to protect me. He can't stand people suffering.'

As for her health generally, she says it is fine. 'Of course there is *possibility* I get cancer; I'm not God! When I hear talk about genetic dangers of radiation, I get strange feeling: I don't like to think about it. I try not to. Those are possibilities, not facts. I say to myself, be sensible! If atomic bomb not fall, I have prettier face. *That's* a fact! My hands are sometimes painful now, but that's arthritis, because I'm getting older. So don't mix that up with bomb!'

On the way back to her house near Manhattan Beach, we stopped at a huge Japanese shopping centre, complete with an enormous supermarket stocked with Japanese foods, Japanese banks, and real estate and travel agents. Shigeko wanted to buy a birthday present for a two-year-old girl she had looked after. She spent some time carefully comparing the patterns of frilly pants before buying two pairs. Next we bought some sweet bean-paste cakes to have with tea. As we drove away, I saw just off the main road, in a row of smaller shops, a hairdresser and beauty parlour with a name that took me aback: in large letters it said HAIROSHI-MA. For all Shigeko's humour and directness, I did not have the nerve to ask her what she thought about it, although I wished later that I had.

Her house was chaotic. She was half-packed for her move, although she did not yet know where she would be moving to. The pictures were still on the walls, and I counted at least six framed photographs of Norman Cousins, several with Shigeko and Norman Jr; the largest picture was an oil painting of Norman and Ellen, smiling out from a heavy gold frame. Also hanging on the wall was a tribute to Shigeko from Senator Edward

156

Kennedy, dated March 1982, thanking her for appearing at a forum in the United States Senate on the dangers of nuclear war. 'You were most eloquent and compelling,' it read. 'I think [your contribution] will have a profound impact on the debate on nuclear arms and reinforce our efforts to prevent another nuclear catastrophe.' Other certificates on display were from the Physicians for Social Responsibility, the Asian Pacific Americans for Nuclear Awareness, and her son's Award of Merit from the Dean of Pepperdine College.

We cleared a space on the sofa and drank tea while I asked her to tell me about her experiences during and immediately after the bombing. After hearing her story, I asked her whether she ever felt angry about what had been done to her. 'No, I feel sad, not angry,' she said. How much did she mind about the scars still visible on her face? 'Not just face. My body is like world map. You want to see England?' She laughed and pulled up her sweater and blouse. There was a long scar down her stomach. 'They take skin for hands from here,' she said. 'First they cut, then they open, then they stretch and stretch and pull' – she mimed a large piece of skin being pulled out and away from her body – 'and cut again and sew together. Place on stomach most painful of all; also legs.' She showed me a large deep scar, like a shallow pit, at the top of one thigh, where an attempt at a skin graft had been made in Tokyo before she went to America. 'Stomach skin on face too,' she said. 'Looks smooth, but feels hard, see?' She took my hand and put it to her lower cheek, which did feel oddly hard and unyielding. 'Not like normal skin,' she went on, drawing my fingers across her inner forearm, where the skin was fine and soft. 'But worst scars now up here.' She touched her chest above her breast. Amazed at her matter-of-fact attitude, I asked her if she had always been so stoical, so unemotional, about a series of wounds and scars that I could not imagine enduring.

She looked at me quizzically. 'I wasn't born an angel, or born stupid,' she said. 'As a young girl in Japan, I had a raw feeling. As you get older, sensitivity different, not shy any more. But my emotions go up and down, natural thing. But like I said, physical pain I forget. God take away. Emotional painful things, feelings, they stay. Every once in a while it flashes in my mind, when I see a pretty girl – I wish I could be like that! Wow! So slim, neat, pretty. Once in a while I feel that way; but feeling doesn't stay long. Too busy. Too busy!' She gave another peal of laughter.

Shigeko struck me as a woman of natural high spirits that none of her experiences had been able to dim; although I heard from one or two people who knew her well in Japan and America that periodically she would collapse into gloom and inertia. Her life in America has been much more free than it would probably ever have been in Japan, but it also seems a little precarious. She told me she has constant money problems; Norman's father has never supported them, and although she has had various jobs as a nurse, in hospitals and privately, she has not managed to build a career. 'I don't like to tie myself down, because I need to be able to travel, when I am asked,' she said rather vaguely. She sees a good bit of the Cousins family, and they have helped her and Norman financially and, she told me, pay for his education. Her devotion to them was striking. 'Mrs Cousins is a really wonderful person, no one knows how wonderful,' said Shigeko fervently. 'And all the girls are so sweet to me, always like sisters. Because Mr Cousins has no son, I think Norman is special to him too. He treats him just like his grandson.' They were both going to the Cousins house the next day for a big family holiday reunion.

Before I left, Shigeko said she would like to cook us some Japanese food. But first, she wanted to show me some photographs of the baby girl she had recently been looking after. She brought out a pile of snaps of a pudgy, naked, beaming baby and gazed dotingly at them with evident pleasure and pride. 'Isn't she so cute? Look at that perfect body,' she said. Some of the pictures showed Shigeko with the child; one was particularly good of her. When I remarked on this, she looked at it almost complacently. 'Yes, sometimes I am very photogenic, I think. And my hands — ' She stretched out her small, slightly contorted hands to show me. 'I can't play piano, but I can do practical things, no problems. I can bathe new-born babies, even.' Had she ever, I wondered, thought of marrying again? 'Never occurred to me!' said Shigeko cheerfully. 'No one asked me! Who wants me?' She gazed around the room in mock enquiry. Then she went to the small kitchen to prepare rice and miso soup. I heard her start to sing: 'You Are My Sunshine', one of the songs the Hiroshima Maidens learned in the mid-1950s and adopted as their own.

15

Forty Years Later

In Hiroshima, I was struck by how reticent people still
are about the darker side of the story of what has
happened to the women who went to the United States
as Maidens during the thirty years since they returned.
No one I spoke to would do more than confirm certain
facts; asked for details, or to analyse causes, they
became forgetful or evasive. Within six years, two of the
women had died. One developed a liver disorder, which
Dr Harada told me might possibly, though he could not
be sure, have been connected with radiation damage.
One is rumoured to have killed herself. I found it
impossible to discover whether she was the woman who
had been so homesick and depressed in New York. One
who married and had a daughter later divorced;
rumours went round that her husband had only married
her because he thought her American family would
support them financially, and when his demands were
not met, he left. In a Japanese television programme
made ten years ago, one of the women spoke of how she
had taken a job in a factory but found the work made
her tire easily as she was very anaemic; another admitted that she was subject to depressions, especially
around the time of the anniversary of the bombing each
August. Most recently, the whole group was saddened
when Suzue, who had trained as a beautician and
opened her own beauty parlour, died of cancer not long
after losing both her husband and one of her daughters.
In any community, out of twenty-four women chosen at

random some are going to have emotional problems, become ill and die during the passage of thirty years; but for that generation, living in Hiroshima, such events can only be looked at rather differently.

The relation between atomic bomb radiation and cancer is complex. Radiation and carcinogenesis have been linked since 1902, soon after the first medical use of X-rays, but in cancer research, to establish cause and effect in statistically convincing terms appears almost impossible. The anxious Hiroshima survivors have been the subject of innumerable surveys on the incidence of cancers of various kinds among them, and the results to date are as confusing as they are frightening, partly because they are so imprecise and open to different interpretations.

It is generally agreed that a direct connection can be made between high doses of radiation and certain cancers, in particular leukaemia. In the early seventies, the rate of leukaemia was seven times higher among survivors than other people. Responsible and authoritative accounts introduce other evidence with cautious phrases: thus cancers of the salivary gland are said to have 'a significant relation to atomic bomb exposure', which also 'elevates the incidence' of lung cancer. Breast cancer appears to occur more often in the exposed than the non-exposed, especially in women exposed between the ages of ten and nineteen. With other cancers, the pattern is less clear, and for people exposed to smaller doses of radiation, like the Hiroshima Maidens, the direct connection between their experiences in 1945 and their health today is very hard to establish.

Of the twenty-four former Maidens, twenty-one remained in or near Hiroshima. Of the three who have since died, two died of cancer; two others are suffering from cancer now. I asked Dr Harada whether this figure, four out of twenty-one, which struck me as

161

alarming, was significant to him. 'I certainly think the incidence of cancer among the Maidens has been exceptionally high,' he said. 'The incidence of breast cancer is about 2 or 3 per cent in the general population; with the Maidens, it is now 10 per cent.' He went on to express caution about cancer statistics, pointing out that different types of cancer have different cycles or incubation periods and many different possible causes; but overall, when pressed, he admitted that in his opinion there is a clear correlation between the bomb and certain types of cancer. In Dr Harada himself, as well as among the women I talked to, I found a puzzling, almost superstitious reluctance to link exposure to the bomb with cancer which could not simply be explained by the complexity of the figures. It was as if admitting a link made cancer more likely. 'I don't want *hibakusha* to feel inferior,' said Dr Harada. 'I don't want anyone in Japan to say, "If you're a survivor you are going to get cancer." I don't want that at all. I don't like that sort of fatalistic mentality.'

In America and Japan I tried to trace how the project had affected the lives of the other people concerned. For Norman Cousins, having Shigeko and Norman Jr as part of his family life has ensured that the Hiroshima Maidens project has never receded into the past, although his preoccupations today seem very different from those of thirty years ago. When I visited him in California, I asked him whether the project had brought the results he had hoped for.

'I think our hopes were very vague,' he said. 'Just that something better was possible for those girls. And our hopes were then exceeded by the response we got from the American people . . . the homes and hearts that were opened, and the generosity that was shown. At the beginning we literally didn't know where the money to fund the project would come from, even though all the doctors and surgeons were donating their services. In the end we had $17,000 left to start another project.'

Soon after he returned from Japan in 1956 Cousins was asked to look into the plight of another group of women victimised by war: these were middle-aged Polish women living in Germany who had been imprisoned by the Nazis in Ravensbrück, where they had been subjected to appalling medical experiments. Since the war they had been trying to get compensation and help from the German government, without success. Again Cousins involved the readers of the *Saturday Review*, and asked the Quakers to find accommodation for the women in the United States, where some of them had relatives and friends. After they had returned to Europe, Cousins kept up the pressure and eventually they were given compensation in line with that received by other concentration camp victims. 'The Ravensbrück project was a direct consequence and dividend of the Maidens project,' said Cousins.

At least twice more in Cousins' long career as an editor he has managed to combine journalism with a humanitarian crusade. In the Sixties, he turned his attention to the work of Albert Schweitzer in the Congo, visited and interviewed him there, produced articles and a book and also encouraged his readers to support Schweitzer's work with lepers. Later, during the Nigerian Civil War, Cousins based an appeal for help for Biafran children on his Hiroshima experiences. He continued to promote World Federalism and to point out the terrible dangers of war, especially nuclear war; he made several return visits to Hiroshima, where in 1964 he was made an Honorary Citizen. He wrote numerous books; he received a steady stream of honorary degrees and awards. His role as a self-appointed prompter of the conscience of the American people was admired by a great many of his readers and supporters, but has been questioned by some observers who discerned a streak of sentimentality in his approach, and a tendency to move on to the next fashionable cause when it arose; but there is no doubt that he has consistently drawn attention to important issues. Now, approaching his seventies, he appears to be looking inwards rather than out; but he is doing so, characteristically, on the grand scale.

The Cousins live nowadays in an attractive house on a spectacular hillside above Beverly Hills. They look out over ridges and canyons dotted with oleanders and cypresses to the mountains beyond the San Fernando Valley. There is a swimming pool on the terrace, a new tennis court carved out of the steep slope behind, and up above the house a circular white building containing Cousins' library, personal archives and study. He has an office on the campus of the University of California in Westwood, about twenty minutes' drive, past film-stars' mansions, down towards the sea. Since 1978 he has been attached to the Faculty of Medicine, setting up and teaching courses in a field more or less invented by himself, known as Medical Humanities. His special interest these days is in what he has called 'the biochemistry of the emotions: the way attitudes and emotions can bring on disease or improve prospects of recovery'. He has written two extremely widely read and debated books on the subject, both based on his own experiences.

In the last ten years he has twice been seriously ill, with a muscular disease and a serious heart condition, and each time decided to eschew conventional medicine and apply his inner resources to the problem. His success in curing himself has appealed to the huge numbers of Americans who are both preoccupied with their health and suspicious of doctors. 'The experts are vulnerable, as I've found in every area of my life,' says

164

Cousins with some satisfaction. He recalled how many 'experts' on Japan, including the State Department, had said that the Hiroshima Maidens project was inadvisable and would never work: 'What those experts were missing was the extent to which love in the United States would be a solvent for all their carefully defined problems. The beautiful intangibles don't weigh as heavily as they should with experts.' So, looking back, did he think that the project had succeeded most on an intangible or emotional level? 'I think we wanted them, from the beginning, to have a magical experience rather than just a medical one. The medicine or surgery became the rationale,' said Cousins. 'We knew we were transporting those young ladies into a new dimension, and we hoped that it would do much to ease their burden.'

Before I left, I reminded Cousins of something he had once written, about the purpose behind his attempts to help victims of the atomic bombings. 'My hope was that Hiroshima might become something of a classroom in which the world's statesmen might be students.'

'That hope still lives,' he said slowly. 'The fulfilment is yet to come.'

From time to time Dr Simon, as one of the surgeons who worked on the Hiroshima Maidens project, has been asked to support anti-war causes. He has always refused, fearing that such campaigns are politically motivated.

During the Vietnam war, he told me, when concern began to mount in America at the number of civilian casualties, it was suggested that victims of napalm should be brought to Mount Sinai for treatment. Both he and Dr Barsky felt that such a gesture was likely to lead to anti-American propaganda. 'The Vietnam war should never have happened,' said Dr Simon fiercely, 'but the anti-war people wanted to exploit burned

children for political reasons and we didn't want anything to do with it.' However, Dr Barsky felt strongly
that something should be done for the casualties. He
helped to design and run an American-funded Children's Hospital in Saigon, opened in 1969 specifically
for the treatment of burns and plastic surgery. 'This was
the crowning achievement of his life,' said Dr Simon
with some emotion. He showed me an appreciation he
had written of Dr Barsky for their professional journal,
Plastic and Reconstructive Surgery, after his death in
1982. 'That passage sums up what he came to believe,
after our experience with the Hiroshima Maidens, and I
agree with him.' The passage reads:

> He believed that in countries where plastic surgery was not
> developed, the civilian population could best be served 1)
> by making the facilities available, 2) by caring for children
> in their own country with parents and loved ones close at
> hand, and 3) by training the local medical profession to
> care for their own people . . . Dr Barsky was emphatic in
> his view that plastic surgery (and all medicine) must be
> a-political − a burned child belongs to all of us.

After the American withdrawal from Saigon in 1975 the
hospital was shut down; Dr Barsky tried in vain to have
it re-opened. During his retirement in the South of
France he made a number of visits to Third World
countries to advise on the treatment of those in need of
plastic surgery.

Every year, Ida and Richard Day send Toyoko a sum of
money to spend on a Christmas party for 'the girls', as
they still call them; and every year one of their favourite
Christmas cards is one showing a coloured photograph
of as many of the group as Toyoko can gather together.
Quite a number of the host parents have died in the last

few years, but among those who are left there is still some contact with Hiroshima. One New Year card from Japan I saw read: 'Hiroshima has changed, but the spirit of Hiroshima Maidens lives on.'

The Teels, who had both Terue and Michiyo living with them for a while, wrote to tell me how they had also looked after one of the Polish women from Ravensbrück; the letter continues:

> More recently Quakers and many other Church groups were involved in taking in refugees from Vietnam and Cambodia, supporting them in many ways until they could get adjusted to life here, find homes and jobs. Our Meeting joined with two others and rather fully supported a family of three for over a year. And now many Meetings and churches are involved in various ways in trying to help those who have fled from Latin American countries. Sometimes this is just contributions to organisations deeply involved in this work, sometimes it is being host families and sometimes (especially very recently) providing sanctuary in homes or churches for these illegal aliens who may be picked up by authorities at any time.
>
> So it continues to be a troubled world with man's inhumanity to man still on the march. We hope the faith which begets acts of mercy will also continue and eventually prove equal to the mounting needs.

'Whether they like it or not, or like me or not, I still worry about them as if they were my daughters,' says Helen Yokoyama of her relationship with the group. To some, though not all, of the women living in Hiroshima, she is still 'sensei' (teacher), someone they turn to for advice and comfort. 'As soon as I hear the voice on the telephone I can tell if all is well or if they are in some trouble,' says Helen.

For the past fourteen years, she has been living in her late husband's family house north of Hiroshima.

167

Although it has a modern kitchen and bathroom tucked away at the back, it is remarkably unaltered from the traditional structure, a fact in which Helen takes some pride. She still prepares the old stone tub heated by a wood fire underneath if a guest prefers a Japanese bath, and she likes to cook over the open hearth in the middle of the old dining hall. The house is wooden, with sloping eaves, clay tiles and paper sliding doors; outside there is raked gravel, a camellia tree and a fine view over rice paddies to a chestnut grove with steep forested hills beyond, inhabited by wild monkeys. Helen lives alone and likes her solitude and independence, although she spends some time in Hiroshima with her younger daughter Ai, who works for the city government. Occasionally the girls, as she also calls them, have been out to stay with her: 'They know they can always come here,' she says.

Helen Yokoyama is well aware of the tensions felt by the women over the past thirty years, and to some extent she is sympathetic. 'Hiroshima certainly didn't welcome them back with open arms,' she says firmly. But she also appears to feel that some of the women have become self-absorbed. Helen Yokoyama, I gathered, feels that because the Maidens received special care they should have felt it their duty ever since to help others. 'What saddens me most,' she said, 'is that along with Japan's economic progress some of them have become quite materialistic. When they didn't have very much, spiritually they were much wealthier. They are bonded together by the spirit of love – they shouldn't be this way!' She had hoped, she said, that more of them would find a way to serve the community, through social work perhaps; only two, however, have chosen that sort of career.

In the end, she too regards the psychological or spiritual benefits of the project as its most important consequence. She told me how one mother, who after the war used to shout curses at American planes flying overhead, and often spoke of her undying hatred for the United States, later said that since her daughter's return from treatment she started each day with a prayer of thanks and blessings for the American people. 'Hate can be turned to love, you know,' said Helen Yokoyama. 'That was the beauty of the project. It all started with the love that was tendered to them. In any difficulty in life, if you know someone really cares for you, it helps, doesn't it? That's what changed things for those girls.'

Dr Harada, within a few years of his return from America to Hiroshima, went through a terrible family tragedy: his wife died of stomach cancer. He thinks, though he cannot be sure, that her illness might have had something to do with the atomic bombing. 'She came in from the suburbs to the ruins of the hospital, near the hypocentre, to dig for medical supplies,' he told me, 'and stayed in the city to take care of her parents who died two weeks later. I suppose she was affected by radiation.' He operated on her himself, but she died the following year, 1961. She was forty-five, and they had four children, two still quite young. Dr Harada was rescued from deep depression after this, he said, by two things; he married again, as his wife had wished, and he began to take a more active part in Hiroshima's peace movement. He also became a leader in the continuing campaign to obtain help for *hibakusha*. 'We doctors in Hiroshima tried to get free treatment for survivors,' he said. 'The government should pay, because the survivors suffered for the rest of the Japanese people. Some think they were punished by heaven for all people on the earth.'

In the early 1960s he helped to set up the World Friendship Centre, a Christian organisation in Hiroshima that provides a base in the city where visitors can meet survivors of the bombing and discuss ways to promote world peace and the anti-nuclear cause. By 1967, he and other Japanese peace activists were becoming concerned about the effects of the Vietnam war on the civilian population; there were rumours and newspaper stories about napalmed villagers and the plight of orphaned children, which reminded Dr Harada of the early years after the bombing of Hiroshima. He felt it was Japan's turn to try to help, and suggested to Norman Cousins that another Japanese-American project might be set up, this time to treat Vietnamese children. At first, Cousins sounded interested; but in the face of official American denials that napalm was being used and the strong suggestion that the Left was exaggerating the plight of the orphans, he dropped the idea. But Dr Harada decided to go to Saigon, to see for himself.

There, by an extraordinary coincidence, he met Dr Barsky, who told him that he too was looking into ways to help civilian casualties. 'I am trying to repay my ten-year-old debt to you by coming to Vietnam now,' Dr Harada said to him. Although both doctors soon discovered that there was indeed a great need of their services, nobody in Saigon at that time seemed keen to take up Dr Harada's proposal that he should take some Vietnamese children back to Hiroshima to be cared for. He visited hospitals and orphanages, confirmed that conditions were bad and there was evidence of napalm burns, and returned to Hiroshima telling his new contacts that if a way could be found to send older casualties to Hiroshima, he and his associates would look after them. Over the next few years a handful of wounded Vietnamese did arrive, and Dr Harada treated them and found them work and homes. There are still, he told me, three crippled Vietnamese men in Hiroshima who call him Papa. An orphanage was built in Saigon from contributions raised in Hiroshima. No one outside Vietnam knows what has happened to it since the Communist takeover.

When I asked Dr Harada what he now, looking back, thinks the Hiroshima Maidens project achieved, he said with conviction, 'For the American people, it was good. It helped them understand what happened in Hiroshima, and encouraged the American peace movement to stand up against nuclear weapons. In Japan it helped us get treatment for survivors. And plastic surgery developed here at a wonderful speed. Now we have almost 1,000 surgeons in our society: then I was the only one. And I myself started to open my eyes internationally and study the peace movement because of the Hiroshima Maidens project.' And how about the women themselves? Did he consider that their treatment had been successful? He paused. 'Yes, but disfigurement caused by keloid scars is very difficult to treat with complete result. Reconstruction of the functions – so that eyes or lips can open and close – can maybe succeed 70 per cent, the cosmetic result maybe only 50 per cent, and each case will vary. And some individuals have very large expectations, others not. In my opinion, from the surgical point of view, the treatment received by the Maidens was maybe 80 per cent successful. That was the best that could be expected. The result in general was larger on the mental side. The Maidens' minds were opened, they felt the goodwill of the Americans, especially the Quakers, and became happier. The most important feature in treatment of *hibakusha* is heart; next comes technique.'

Dr Harada has said that he wishes that some of the former Maidens still living in Hiroshima would play some public part in working for world peace. This view reflects his own strong feelings that Hiroshima should take the lead in drawing world attention to the horrors of nuclear weapons. 'To work for world peace is a duty!' he said. 'Many Hiroshima people feel so. We think all human beings are *hibakusha*, everybody.' He showed me something he had written: 'The *hibakusha* have looked into the mouth of hell and have said: "It makes no difference whether it be America or the Soviet Union. This must not happen to human beings again." '

As I was leaving, I admired a bowl of late roses on a low table. I had been told that Dr Harada loves roses and has bred new varieties. 'Yes, I have made two new roses,' he said. 'I have called one Miyajima and the other Ota River. The name of Hiroshima is not good enough for a rose.'

16

In Hiroshima Now

A well-worn joke is told in Hiroshima. It concerns an anxious foreign visitor, probably an American, who asks a taxi-driver on arrival: How are things in Hiroshima these days? The taxi-driver shakes his head mournfully and says: Terrible. The carp have never been so bad. The visitor immediately thinks — the bomb! radiation! the fish are still affected — and is suffused with guilt. But the taxi-driver is referring to the fortunes of the Carp, the famous Hiroshima baseball team, nowadays the city's obsession.

When I arrived in Hiroshima in search of the former Hiroshima Maidens, the Carp were in fact doing extremely well, having come top of both regional and national leagues that season, but the lesson of the story still held. Most visitors to Hiroshima feel uneasy, at best, about the city's past; the atomic explosion is the most famous event in its history, and the Peace Memorial Park, with its museum and monuments, its number one tourist attraction. But whereas outsiders walk through the Peace Park quietly and reverently, thinking bleak thoughts about the terrible past and the terrifying future, the people of Hiroshima go to stroll with their friends, sweethearts and babies, admire the flowers, feed the pigeons and ride their bikes. Foreigners are often seen standing tearfully by the Memorial Cenotaph or the burned out Dome of the Industrial Promotion Hall, left in ruins (although carefully shored up and preserved against collapse) as a warning; the Japanese pose in

173

Japan and America, 1956–85

front of them, smiling cheerfully for holiday snaps. To the outsider, especially if, like me, you have been studying the events of August 1945, it is impossible, at first, to look at the flowerbeds and river-banks without seeing vivid images of the burned and bleeding people who died and suffered there. What must it be like, you wonder, to live on in the place you saw almost obliterated, where your friends and family were wounded and died, where you yourself were scarred and changed for ever?

It is instructive to feel how rapidly such thoughts quieten and recede. Within days, even while concentrating on learning more details of the terrible past, I was beginning to appreciate the pleasures of Hiroshima's present. No one encouraged me to do so more than the people I had come to see; far from wanting me to focus my attention on their suffering, they told me about good restaurants and shops, urged me to visit local beauty spots, brought me presents of guidebooks and maps and locally-made souvenirs.

The rebuilt Hiroshima is not beautiful; in fact, like much of modern industrialised Japan, it is positively ugly; with forests of overhead wires, garish neon signs and hectic traffic. But it is busy and thriving, and the people crowd into the shops and arcades, and enjoy eating out. The shellfish, the local speciality, is excellent. Down by the station old men in aprons open oysters at high speed and pack them in cardboard boxes with seaweed for travellers to take as presents.

Against this agreeable background I tried to focus on the past, asking women to talk to me about their scars, physical and emotional. I had been warned, by the only journalist then to have interviewed the Hiroshima Maidens in recent years and himself a *hibakusha*, that many of them would be likely to refuse to see me and that those who did might be reticent. He had tried over a

174

period of months to contact all eighteen in the Hiroshima area, and had been rebuffed by eleven, a response that he found puzzling and painful. But six women agreed, without too much hesitation, to see me. I knew that these women were the ones whose feelings about their experiences in America and afterwards are the most positive. Some of the others, I learned, fear publicity and do not want any more attention. To some observers, including the *hibakusha* journalist, this indicated a saddening reversion to the insecurity and shame they had felt as girls before going to America; they are still hiding, he thinks, and have not yet come to terms with what happened to them. Oddly, I seemed to find it easier than he did to imagine why such women, who have been through so much, and whose main aim must have been to be allowed to build as ordinary a life as possible, without being singled out by their scars or anything else, would want to be left alone and not to have to answer questions. To be able to turn away from the past and live, or seem to live, as if terrible events, public or private, have never happened can seem like evasion or cowardice, but can also be a form of courage. I felt unable either to put pressure on the women who preferred to remain silent, or to assume that their preference necessarily meant they were less happy or secure than the others.

The women I met in Hiroshima talked to me, I felt, not because they particularly wanted to but because they felt they should; they consider it a duty to express their gratitude for what was done for them thirty years ago in America. Their lack of bitterness or resentment at what had happened to them in 1945 amazed me.

Through them, and the other survivors I met and read about, I began to perceive something of the curious and painful position of the *hibakusha* today. As individuals trying to cope with everyday life, they very often want to be able to leave their terrible past behind. It is not easy to be a symbol of something as appalling as nuclear war, to see people's expressions change as they look at you and wonder if you are really as normal as you seem. One *hibakusha* told me that when he was asked to appear on a European television programme not long ago he received the clear impression that his hosts were disappointed by his ordinary appearance. Of course no survivor of the bombing can forget what happened, and none of them wants the rest of the world to be allowed to forget it either; but they have found through bitter experience that their *hibakusha* identity can bring them extra problems. Many of them try to conceal their past, as there is some evidence that employers are wary of taking them on. Their marriage prospects, or nowadays those of their children, can also be affected. One man told me he had been lucky that his children's in-laws had not raised objections when they learned of his exposure to the bomb; he is working now on a study of discrimination against *hibakusha* in Japanese society.

As well as all the fearful physical after-effects, *hibakusha* have learned to beware of the draining psychological damage that obsession with the past can cause. This sense of being permanent victims has been called in Hiroshima 'leukaemia of the spirit' and 'keloid of the heart', and it seemed to me that the former Hiroshima Maidens I met were determined to avoid it. Their awareness of having been luckier than most through their American experiences had helped them sustain a positive, cheerful line.

Only one of the former Maidens living in Hiroshima has taken any active part in campaigning for peace or publicising the horrors of nuclear war, and she has only done so comparatively recently. All the women I met shared the suspicions of other *hibakusha* at the rows and political manoeuvrings of the organised peace parties during the Sixties and Seventies; anti-Americanism did not appeal to them, and their experiences with the press made them fearful of appearing or speaking in public. But one of the women who was rejected for the project, Miyoko, has been deeply involved with the peace movement, both through her work as a librarian at the Peace Memorial Library, alongside the Peace Museum, and through her friendship with Barbara Reynolds, an American woman activist who lived in Hiroshima for many years, once sailed a boat on to the Pacific Test Zone and helped to organise the Peace Pilgrimages around the world.

Miyoko's work involves collecting and cataloguing writing from Japan and all over the world about atomic and nuclear war, and sending out information. She has travelled several times with the exhibition organised by the Museum of drawings and paintings by survivors of how they remember 6 August 1945; thus she spends each day at close quarters with the moving and dreadful relics of the event. Near the library are constantly running films of the explosion, glass cases full of keloids in bottles, stained and torn clothes and children's charred schoolbooks. Miyoko appeared to be the most vulnerable of the women I saw, although she is less visibly scarred than many of the Maidens. Her work for peace is obviously of vital personal importance to her. She has twice been to the United States on speaking tours, and while I was in Hiroshima I saw a film made during one of them. Miyoko looks and speaks in the film like someone at the limit of her physical and emotional strength. She weeps as she describes in halting English what she has been through; the effect on the American audiences (mostly of young people) was evident.

'I don't want anyone else ever to experience what I did,' she told me, tears filling her eyes. 'That's why I am

177

giving my story, even though I am very tired of looking back, and find it very difficult. I have nightmares, and my classmates who died appear in my dreams. They encourage me; that's why I keep on.'

Many *hibakusha* find such display of themselves and use of their experiences profoundly antipathetic, even distasteful. Certainly for most of the women I met, it would be unthinkable. In different ways most of them said the same thing: their way of working for peace is to live their ordinary lives.

For two or three of them, including Hiroko, who married the American and whose face is still a shock to look at, it is rather different. 'I don't have to make speeches, tell my story to journalists,' she said stoutly. 'Every day I meet people; they ask me what happened to my face. I tell them. That's working for peace, for me! Please tell true story!'

Underneath, I sensed that all the women have the same fear: that despite the years of good health, the absence of clear statistics indicating that *hibakusha* have more illnesses, get more cancers, die younger than the rest of us, one day they will fall ill as a result of the explosion forty years ago. Nobody quite knows, and everybody wonders. Toyoko, who has already been ill herself possibly as a result of radiation, tried to explain.

'Illness — better not to think about it! We don't like to tell people if we feel ill, because they think it must be because of the atomic bomb. All the girls, I think, when we are young we don't worry because we were so healthy. But from middle age, and now, we start to have problems and to worry; but we still don't like to think it might be because of the bomb. One of us, who married and had a daughter, and now has grandchildren, she feels that way. She doesn't come to our group meetings, because she doesn't want to be reminded that her daughter is second generation survivor. We who are

178

single people don't have that kind of problem, but we still don't want to think too much about it. In Hiroshima, if you are ill, neighbours think it is because you were in the atomic bombing; that's why I would prefer to live in Tokyo; nobody knows.'

Toyoko looked bleak as she spoke. I asked if she felt depressed and anxious much of the time. Immediately she pulled herself together. 'Oh no! I always find some happiness in things. I think I never give up, I guess. Many of us girls are strong and happy in ourselves.' Did she still feel anger at the way her life had been changed? 'Oh yes. But this is war you see, what war is like. Our group, when we get together, we always say — if war comes again — I don't know — we should just run, escape to the mountains. I don't know where, but I not stay in this city.'

'But . . .' I started to say. She looked at me, half-laughing, self-mocking, struggling through her awkward English to tell me what she meant.

'I know now, it's different. Different type of war.' She paused. 'No place to go.'

Postscript

There is still argument about the number of people killed by the atomic bomb dropped over Hiroshima in August 1945. Figures range between 70,000 (the lowest estimate for those killed instantly) and 300,000 (including soldiers, other temporary residents of the city and those who have died subsequently as a result of the bombing). The most widely accepted figures, according to a report prepared for the United Nations by the city of Hiroshima, are that 140,000 people were dead as a direct consequence of the bomb by the end of 1945, and that 50,000 more died by the end of 1950.

According to the Health and Welfare Ministry in Tokyo, about 370,000 people exposed to the atomic bombs at Hiroshima and Nagasaki are living in Japan today. These people are registered as *hibakusha* and entitled to free medical treatment. The average age of *hibakusha* is now over sixty. The Confederation of Atomic and Hydrogen Bomb Sufferers said recently that 'in old age, their loneliness and anxiety about their health have increased'. In a sample of 200 elderly *hibakusha*, 40 per cent said that they had no friends who could understand their sufferings.

Since the Hiroshima A-Bomb Hospital opened in 1956, 8,361 survivors have been admitted. By mid-1984, 1,749 had died. In 1983, 468 new patients were admitted, of whom 54 died. Their average age was seventy, and 36.1 per cent of them had been exposed to radiation within 2 kilometres of the explosion in 1945.

22 per cent of them were admitted to the hospital after they developed malignant tumours.

Scientists are still debating the precise nature of the radiation emitted by the bombs dropped at Hiroshima and Nagasaki and revising their estimates of the dosage received by survivors. Since 1975 the Atomic Bomb Casualty Commission has been superseded by the Radiation Effects Research Foundation, funded equally by the governments of the United States and Japan. Research still continues into the relation between exposure to the bombings and cancers of the bones, tissues and blood. Genetic evidence will be scrutinised for generations to come. More work is called for on the psychological, emotional and social after-effects.

The Confederation of Atomic and Hydrogen Bomb Sufferers Organisations last year conducted a major survey of 3,690 survivors, of whom 1,739 were women. 62 per cent of them expressed 'deep anxiety' about their health, their future, and the genetic inheritance they have bequeathed to their descendants.

Note on Sources

For the facts about the bombing of Hiroshima and ⬛⬛⬛⬛⬛ ⬛e afterwards I have relied on *Hiroshima and N⬛⬛⬛⬛⬛⬛ ⬛e Physical, Medical and Social Effects of the Ato⬛⬛⬛ ⬛⬛⬛⬛⬛g,* by the Committee for the Compilation of ⬛⬛⬛⬛⬛⬛⬛⬛ ⬛n Damage Caused by the Atomic Bombs in Hiroshima and Nagasaki, published in Japan by Iwanami Shoten, Tokyo, 1979, and in the United States (translated by Eisei Ishikawa and David L. Swain) by Basic Books, New York, 1981.

I also consulted Professor Joseph Rotblatt of the University of London and Dr Scott Davis of the Radiation Effects Research Foundation on the nature and effects of radiation. I am grateful to them for their advice; any mistakes or misinterpretations are my responsibility.

I have also used the following books and occasionally quoted short passages from them:

CHUJO, KAZUO. *The Nuclear Holocaust,* Asahi Shimbun, Tokyo, 1983.

——*The Hiroshima Maidens,* Asahi Shimbun, Tokyo, 1984.

COUSINS, NORMAN. *Present Tense,* McGraw-Hill, New York, 1967.

HARADA, TOMIN. *Hiroshima Surgeon,* Faith and Life Press, Newton, Kansas, 1983.

HERSEY, JOHN. *Hiroshima,* Knopf, New York, 1946.

JUNGK, ROBERT. *Children of the Ashes,* Heinemann, London, 1961.

LIFTON, ROBERT JAY. *Death in Life,* Basic Books, New York, 1967.

NAKAMOTO, HIROKO. *My Japan 1930-1951,* McGraw-Hill, New York, 1970.

PACIFIC WAR RESEARCH SOCIETY. *The Day Man Lost,* Kodansha, Tokyo, 1981.